Médecins Sans Frontières

Voices from the Silence

Testimonies from Angola

MEDECINS SANS FRONTIERES
DOCTORS WITHOUT BORDERS

Cover photo © Thomas Roy. Caala 2001.

Published by Médecins Sans Frontières
March 2004
720 Spadina Ave., Suite 402
Toronto, Ontario M5S 2T9 Canada

Voices from the Silence - Testimonies from Angola
ISBN 0-9733309-1-0

Our thanks

to all of the Angolans who shared their stories with us.

May the physical wounds be a thing of the past

and the psychological wounds be allowed to heal.

We dedicate this book to a better future for the people of Angola.

Médecins Sans Frontières
Angola. 2004

Contents

Map of Angola

♀
24 years old
Mussende
March 2003

I was born in Caluquembe, in Huila Province. I left there when I was four years old. I've never been back. I was captured in 1983 by the soldiers of UNITA who took me to [UNITA's headquarters in] Jamba, where I grew up, in the bush. In Jamba they handed me over to a house of the party. A house of the party is where they put the children who have no relatives. Those children are used to doing lots of work for the party, they carry material to the front-lines, like this (shows how to carry things on top of her head), where the soldiers are. There were many children there who were captured and lots of men and women as well who were also cap-tured. I didn't like living there because they enslaved me. Today I am 24 years old but I've never studied anything. Now, this year, I am studying in the fourth class [of primary school]. They just used me to work for them and they never put me in school. Today I am backwards because of them. There were lots of schools in Jamba, but it was only the children whose parents were in UNITA who could study. I didn't have the luck to meet someone who would put me in school.

I grew up in Jamba. In 1996, during that small peace, we went to Bailundo. Then we left there and went to Negage. I crossed the whole country on foot. Then in 1998 we were in Caculama, but the government administration arrived so we had to withdraw. We went back into the bush and came here, to Mussende. The other people I was with, they died. There was an attack. Look, (pulls up her skirt to show a scar running the whole way down the outside of her right thigh) this was from a bomb. It was shrapnel from a MIG [fighter plane]. The MIG dropped a bomb and it broke me here, and the others were all cut up and they died. And here, (shows scars on the back of her right knee) these were bullets. This happened in Cangandala. We were carrying material to there, UNITA was preparing an attack, but we ran into a government offensive. That was our bad luck. The others, one was from Quibala, one was from Gabela, one was from Sumbe. They all died, they were hit in the head. That was in 2000. We'd all been captured by UNITA. We were living in the bush, under the trees. We didn't have a fixed place where we stayed. If it rained sometimes we could make a shelter and go in there. But if things were going badly we just had to keep walking under the rain. There was a UNITA surgeon in the bush who treated my leg. My leg was broken; inside here there is a plate. He put it in, in the bush. We didn't have any anaesthetic or painkillers or anything, he just did it, with nothing, in the open air. Now I can walk, I can run, but soon I will have to take this plate out. After this happened I couldn't walk for a year. The others had to make a stretcher out of sticks to carry me until I got better.

When the war ended I was here, in Zone 3, which is an area four days walk from Mussende. We were suffering a lot there. We ate badly, we slept badly. The children all got anaemia. When my leg was injured, I already had my son, he was a little baby. He was born in the rain and they cut his umbilical cord with grass. As soon as he was born, I had to tie him on my back and carry on walking. Soon afterwards his father died and left me alone with this small baby. He was a UNITA soldier, he died in an attack. I had to get married. UNITA only respected women if they had a husband who could protect them. I had no one there, no family, so I had to join up with someone to treat me well and respect me. So I married with my son's father but, unfortunately, he died in 2001. In 2001, the war was much closer, much worse. There was lots of death, lots of hunger, lots of rain, we suffered a lot. When we heard there was peace we didn't believe it. It wasn't until a helicopter came from the Angolan Armed Forces (FAA) to collect [UNITA] General Kananai, and then he came back and gave a lecture, and then we started coming out of the bush to come here. The people in the bush didn't believe that [UNITA leader] Savimbi was dead. Lots of them still don't believe it, until today. I believed it because I saw the films of his body here in Mussende. I felt a lot when I knew he was dead because it was him that took everybody by force. I thought, now that he's dead it means that we can stop dying. He died, and the peace came. I didn't feel very sorry about his death because it was because of him that I suffered, it was because of him that I didn't go to school, it was because of him that I don't know my mother or father, until now. I live alone, just with my little boy. If it weren't for UNITA I would be with my parents, I would be someone, I would have people. But they took me from my people to destroy me.

After the peace arrived I went to the demobilisation camp here but on the sixth day I left there because I saw that there was no point in my staying there. So I came here to Mussende town. At that time I was still in mourning for my husband. I was very thin. I convinced someone to give me a job as a cook. I don't know how to find my family. I've been separated from them for 20 years. I don't know what they're like, what they're called, I don't know anything. Some people say my mother's called Idalina, others say my father's called Henrique. I'm just a big question mark. I don't know what to do about my life. The worst thing in the war was eating badly, living in the rain, climbing up and down mountains. We were living like wild animals. We didn't have any time to rest; we just had to keep walking. The government had prepared a good offensive to finish us off in the bush and we were really suffering. We were wearing sacks. We would beat the trees to take off the bit under the bark to make material to carry the babies. It was awful. My life has changed a lot since the peace came and I started working. Today I sleep on a mattress, and I sleep in peace, even if it's only in a grass hut. Before I couldn't sleep, life was just walking, walking, walking, up mountains like this (indicates a very steep slope with her arm). Big mountains. But since the peace everything is changing. I don't have to carry heavy things on my head any more, I can eat good food. My life is already getting better and will get better still.

I still feel the effects of the war a lot. Today I see people who didn't live in the bush, who lived normal lives with their parents, who are younger than me but they've already studied, and they can do good jobs. But because I can't read or write, all because of the war, I don't know anything, nothing, except for cooking. I'm really behind for my age. If I'd had parents, I could have studied, but UNITA destroyed everything in my life. If I could read and write it would be easy for me to find my parents because I could send letters, but I can't, I don't know anything. What am I going to do with my life? This weighs on me a lot. If I could read I could get a better job, but so long as I can't read I'm condemned to be someone's slave until I can't take it any longer. When I think about this, it hurts a lot.

Nowadays I only have good dreams. In the beginning I only dreamed about the war, but these last three or four months I've only been dreaming about nice things. And I'm not so jumpy any more. Before I used to get shocked, like when aeroplanes flew over, I got very scared. But now I don't any more because the planes which come to destroy, they make a different sound. I think this peace has come to stay. The peace of '92 and '96 was doubtful, it was a sort of peace but people didn't stop preparing for war. But this peace now, even before they signed the peace accords, they silenced the guns. That makes me believe that this is real peace. The only thing that could make another war here is that the government is paying some of the men in the demobilisation camps, and not paying others. And that's creating problems. The ones who aren't paid are complaining, and saying, "We've all been fighting in the bush; we've all suffered the same. How come we don't all get treated the same?" A few weeks ago some of them went to a village, four hours' march from here, and they made confusion and stole the people's things. And when they were captured by the police they said it was because they hadn't been paid and they were angry. That could start another war. People still have that anger in them. And I can understand that because if I met the person who captured me and took me from my parents, I'd be capable of killing him because today I'm like this because of him. My parents had nothing to do with the war. Why would you take an innocent child, only four years old, away from her parents and force her into such a hard life? At least my son won't have to walk and walk in the bush.

"I am already old and tired…I expect nothing more from this life, or from anybody. The only thing I can say is that I wish that this [war] would stop one day. But I've already been hoping for that for 30 years, so you end up believing that it will never end, that's just the way that it is."

— Woman. Caala. September 2000.

The Origins of this Book

The people of Angola were trapped in the hell of war for 40 years: warfare for independence; warfare for the sake of the Cold War powers; warfare for greed and power. Cumulatively Angola's wars have decimated the country. Forty years of fear and brutality have left terrible psychological, social and physical scars on much of the population. Out of a total of around 12 million Angolans, over 4 million were forced out of their homes and left living as "internally displaced persons" (IDPs) – refugees in their own country. A further 450,000 gave up trying to survive in Angola and sought refuge in neighbouring countries. Ten percent of all Angolan children have been separated from their parents and are being brought up by strangers. Nearly half of Angola's children have been left stunted by a lifetime without adequate food. This suffering is not simply an unfortunate side-effect of the fighting; it is in large part the direct and avoidable result of deliberate strategies adopted by the two warring parties.[1]

MSF has been working in Angola for over 20 years: for 15 years of war, for four years of "neither war nor peace", and now for two years of peace. In that time MSF has been working in 16 of the 18 provinces across the country, providing health care and intensive nutritional care to hundreds of thousands of people. By working with some of those most affected by the conflict, MSF has borne witness to the unmaking of a country, the deconstruction of a society, and the traumatisation of a people. Millions have been

---

[1] For more background information, see "Background: 40 Years of War" and chronology in Annex 1.

chased from their homes and pushed to the brink of starvation in a land of plenty. Preventable diseases such as measles and polio, along with treatable diseases such as malaria have obliterated and devastated generations who could have been saved with simple vaccinations and treatment in what has been arguably the worst landmine infestation on the planet.

In the final years of Angola's war the scale of the suffering inflicted by the warring parties, and the price paid by the civilians, became so infuriating that we strengthened our advocacy efforts alongside our medical assistance to the victims of the war. In order to speak out on behalf of the populations, we sought to better understand their tide of hunger and misery. This began with talking to the people. Holed up in a handful of cities, we had no access to the vast battle zones. The best we could do was to listen to the accounts of those who managed to escape from these "grey areas" where the fighting took place. In listening, we sought also to bear witness to the awful predicament of the people trapped by this conflict, in which the outside world had become so complicit. Most of those who spoke to us did not support the fighting, many could not even explain what it was about, but they felt powerless to stop it.

This book has emerged from our conversations with hundreds of Angolans. In it we bring together accounts from men, women and children, from every part of Angola, giving voice to their experiences of Angola's war. Theirs are voices that are rarely heard, even within Angola. They relate a catalogue of horrors. They speak of their fears, their pain, their losses, and their hopelessness. They reveal their physical and mental suffering, as well as their physical and mental fortitude. They convey the weary sadness of grandparents who have been forced to watch as first their children, and then their grandchildren, grow up knowing nothing but war. And they afford us a glimpse into a world that for the duration of the war was largely unseen and largely ignored, by the international community – a world in which the unacceptable became normality.

The stories in this book were recorded between January 2000 and October 2003, and represent a much larger collection. They were gathered by MSF staff working with Angolans in Angola, as well as with Angolan refugees living in camps within Zambia. Most were taken from MSF beneficiaries – patients in our clinics, recipients of our food aid, parents whose children were undergoing intensive nutritional care in our feeding centres. They are not a scientifically selected sample, chosen to reflect the full cross-section of Angolan experience and opinion. Rather, they represent those populations helped by MSF, in various places and at various times during the conflict. Different interviewers used different techniques, but the essential methodology was to listen to the people, to allow them to tell their stories as they saw fit. They are printed here anonymously, to protect all those who shared their stories with us from possible repercussions. We have only identified them by gender, and by when and where they spoke to us. Some of these testimonies were taken during the war, from those who had managed to run away from it. Some could not be recorded until after the war had ended and humanitarian agencies had finally gained access to the millions of Angolans who were trapped in the bush. Those in the final section were taken in the first years after the end of the fighting, to record how Angolans feel about the peace, and to hear of their tentative hopes for the future. In each part the stories are presented in random historical order, starting with stories from older people and finishing with some children's experiences.

We have arranged the main body of the book in three parts, to help the reader make some sense of this senseless conflict. The war has lasted for so long, and affected all Angolans in so many ways, that the lines between these sections are blurred. However we have broadly divided the stories as follows: those people who experienced the war in areas controlled by the MPLA government; those who experienced it within UNITA areas; and those who found themselves trapped between the forces of the two belligerents, at the mercy of both. In most cases political affiliation has been more an accident of geography, than a question of personal choice. The book ends with a final section of testimonies taken after the cease-fire, bringing together impressions from all three of these population groups.

Background: 40 Years of War

Angola has been a veritable laboratory of war, enduring three distinct phases, and every conceivable kind of conflict – international and civil, guerrilla and conventional, wars motivated by nationalism, by ideology and by greed. Fighting began in 1961, when nationalist movements launched the struggle for independence from Portugal. Following independence in 1975 the conflict did not end, but was subsumed into the Cold War. Rival nationalist groups – the Popular Movement for the Liberation of Angola (*Movimento Popular de Libertação de Angola* – MPLA), and the National Union for the Total Independence of Angola (*União Nacional para a Independência Total de Angola* – UNITA) – were adopted as proxies by the superpowers. With support from the Soviet Union and Cuba the MPLA established a single-party, socialist government based in the capital Luanda. Bolstered by financial and technical support from the United States, and military support from apartheid South Africa, UNITA fought to dislodge the MPLA government. The ensuing civil war continued until May 1991, at its height raging in 15 of the country's 18 provinces, and pitting 50,000 Cuban troops against the elite units of the South African armed forces. Predominantly fought between conventional armies in the countryside, the Cold War era conflict wrought havoc on Angola's infrastructure and left the country infested with landmines, but its impact on the civilian population was less grave than during subsequent phases of the war.

With the end of the Cold War the superpowers withdrew

their support and, in 1991, the MPLA and UNITA signed the Bicesse Peace Accords, briefly ending the fighting. The peace agreement called for a cease-fire, demobilisation of the two armies and the creation of a bipartisan Angolan Armed Forces (*Forças Armadas Angolanas* – FAA), the holding of democratic elections, and the establishment of a UN mission to observe the process. The elections went ahead in September 1992, despite the failure to complete the demobilisation process. In the presidential ballot MPLA President José Eduardo dos Santos won 49.57 percent of the vote against 40.07 percent for UNITA leader Jonas Savimbi. In the legislature the MPLA won 54 percent against UNITA's 34 percent. UNITA disputed these results and accused the MPLA of vote rigging.

On October 31, 1992, fighting broke out in Luanda between UNITA and MPLA supporters. By the time it was over on November 3, the battle for Luanda had claimed tens of thousands of lives and driven UNITA out of the capital. Within days UNITA's disciplined army had captured over half of the country from the government forces. Significantly, they captured the country's immensely rich diamond fields, in the north eastern

2002 © Sebastiao Salgado/amazonas images

Between November 2001 and March 2002 famine and disease caused the death of about 4000 children in Chipindo. Chipindo 2002.

Lunda provinces. For the next 10 years UNITA funded its war effort with the sale of diamonds, while the MPLA responded by using the proceeds from Angola's rapidly growing petroleum industry. Angola's natural wealth thus served to fuel its descent into abject poverty.

Rather than being merely a resumption of the Cold War conflict, Angola's post- electoral war marked an entirely new phase in the fighting, with catastrophic consequences for the civilian population. The two armies, the government's FAA and UNITA's FALA (*Forças Armadas para a Libertação de Angola*) faced each other head on, without the cushion of the Cuban and South African armies. Set piece battles in the countryside were replaced by bloody struggles to capture and control the most populated areas. The war became a war of the cities, and civilians became the chief targets and casualties. Fighting focused on those provincial capitals where government forces were still holding out. Hundreds of thousands of civilians found themselves trapped in cities like Malange and Luena, besieged on all sides by UNITA forces. The bombardment, and the resultant hunger and sickness, meant that by October 1993, when aid workers reached Malange for the first time since the elections, MSF found that between 1,000 and 1,500 children were starving to death in the city each month. An MSF report covering 1993 stated "The situation in Malange was indescribable: people trying to survive by eating the leaves of the hedges, thousands of starving children roaming the city streets. They lost their parents during the war. No food had come in since April."[2]

The situation was at its most violent in the cities of Huambo and Cuito, in UNITA's traditional heartland. In the upheaval following the elections both cities had been occupied half by UNITA forces and half by government forces. In the following months both sides shelled each other's positions relentlessly in a bid to force the opposition to abandon these cities. In Huambo this shelling lasted for the notorious "55 days" during which time 15,000 civilians are believed to have been killed. After 55 days the government forces gave in and withdrew 250 kilometres to Benguela on the coast. Tens of thousands of civilians left with the

---

[2] Médecins Sans Frontières, *Annual Report*, 1993, Amsterdam: MSF, 1994, p. 16

government forces and made the long journey on foot to the relative safety of Benguela. In once beautiful Huambo, no single building was left unscarred by the siege. In Cuito the situation was even worse. The frontline ran down the city's main street. The two parties bombed each other across this divide for nine months before agreeing to a cease-fire. During that time no aid or supplies could get into the city, and no civilians could get out. 25,000 people are believed to have died during the siege of Cuito.

After two years of fighting the post-electoral war ended with the signing of the Lusaka Peace Protocol on November 20, 1994. The Lusaka Protocol provided for: a new cease-fire, the establishment of a large UN peacekeeping force, a second demobilization process, and the participation of UNITA in government.

Implementation of the accords proceeded painfully slowly. Both parties committed numerous cease-fire violations, and used the lull in fighting to rearm their forces. The Lusaka Peace Process lasted for three and a half years of what Angolans refer to as "neither war nor peace" or "the lying peace." From March 1998 onwards violent attacks again proliferated throughout the country, and UNITA took back control over dozens of towns handed over to the government during the peace process. From September 1998 the government broke off all dialogue and contact with UNITA, vowing never to negotiate with Jonas Savimbi again. The international community further enforced the ostracisation of UNITA by imposing UN sanctions on the movement, effectively making it illegal to trade or even talk with UNITA. Henceforth, for the duration of the conflict, all humanitarian actors, including aid agencies, UN agencies, MSF and the International Committee of the Red Cross, were unable to work in UNITA-held areas. They had no idea how, or even whether, the civilians in those areas were surviving. The last, post-Lusaka, phase of Angola's civil war officially began in the first week of December 1998, when the Government responded to UNITA provocation by bombarding UNITA's headquarters at Andulo and Bailundo, in the central highlands.

In December, 1998 President dos Santos assured the nation that the "last war for peace" would be over in two months. In the end, it lasted more than three years, inflicting a terrible toll on the civilian population. Both armies' strategies centred upon controlling civilians. For their survival, UNITA's forces had always depended on civilians, who provided the movement with food, sex, labour and recruits. From 1998 to 2002 the FAA fought to deny this civilian support to UNITA, while UNITA fought to retain it. Both armies forced hundreds of thousands of civilians to abandon their homes and to move to areas under their control. When this tactic failed, both armies regularly resorted to killing those who would not follow them. By the beginning of 2002 the FAA had taken the upper hand in the fighting by depopulating vast swathes of Angola's countryside. The populations they forcibly displaced were herded into towns and cities where many thousands starved because they were denied access to their fields and provided with no alternative food source. In their turn those populations left in the bush with UNITA, cut off from their source of food, also starved. The operations of humanitarian agencies like MSF were confined to a few key government-controlled cities and towns for the duration of the conflict. For strategic reasons both belligerents, at different times, refused to allow us to reach and help many of these forcibly displaced civilians. The war only ended when UNITA's founder and leader, Jonas Savimbi, was killed in battle on February 22, 2002. His deputies, themselves on the verge of dying of starvation, moved for peace within days of his death. A third, and hopefully final, peace process has ensued.

"The government does nothing for the people of Angola. They just take the money for the school and hospital and put it in their pockets.... This is the way it is here in Angola. They just use the people to fight the war."

– Man. Matala. February 2001.

Part I
The Government's War

Those Angolans who have lived through the war in government-controlled territory have found themselves targeted in UNITA attacks, and manipulated and abandoned by the government authorities.

As the following stories reveal, until 1991 conditions in MPLA territory were relatively normal. The health care and education systems functioned. Malnutrition was never a major problem. The MPLA army, known as the FAPLA (*Forças Armadas Para a Libertação de Angola*) were paid and equipped, and as a result did not have too abusive a relationship with the civilian population. The MPLA ran the country along strongly authoritarian lines. Even now, over a decade after the official dismantling of the one-party system, the influence of this authoritarian system is still strongly felt. Interviewees speak constantly of "waiting for orders from the government" and "waiting for the government to decide" before being able to take the most basic decisions about their lives, like for example where to live.

From 1991 onwards conditions in MPLA areas deteriorated. The one party system was officially dismantled, although the MPLA retained absolute power. Governmental corruption burgeoned and investment in social services slumped to record lows, civil servants and even the army went unpaid for months at a time, and the health and education systems atrophied. Between 1997 and 2001 the MPLA authorities devoted an average of 3.3 percent of government expenditure to the health sector, and 4.7 percent to the education sector. This equated to spending just nine dollars a year on health care and 13 dollars a year on education for every Angolan.[3]   In the same period an average of 34 percent of the national budget was spent on the war. This led to a situation where, by 2001, one in every four Angolan children living in government-controlled areas died before their fifth birthday; almost half were too short for their age due to chronic malnutrition; and over 40 percent never attended school. Using data gathered exclusively in government-controlled areas, UNICEF declared Angola to be "the worst place in the world to be a child" in 1999.[4]

Conditions in government-controlled areas were made even worse by the way the war was fought. From 1992 UNITA held sway in most of Angola's vast countryside, and concentrated on pinning the government down in a few towns and cities. Anyone perceived by UNITA to have collaborated with the government – including teachers, health workers, traditional chiefs or *sobas*, and any family with a relative in the police, army or "Civil Defence" militias – were singled out and executed in UNITA attacks. Road travel in between the government-held towns was made prohibitively risky by UNITA ambushes and landmines. For years only the truly desperate travelled by road. The rural economy died as fields became battlefields, and what little was produced could not be transported to market. Prices of even the most basic commodities soared. As food became less available and more expensive, malnutrition rates began to climb, especially in the towns and cities of the interior.

Nevertheless, from 1992 onwards, the civilian population increasingly gravitated towards the government-controlled towns and cities leading to a situation where, by 2000, an estimated eighty percent of the population were living in the twenty or so percent of the country under MPLA control. Initially they came fleeing the demands and danger of UNITA. Subsequently, from 1998 onwards, they came also under orders from the Angolan Armed Forces (FAA). As part of their strategy to depopulate UNITA territory the FAA forced hundreds of thousands of villagers to abandon their homes and move into the urban areas. Their houses and crops were often burnt to prevent them from returning home. The testimonies con-

---

[3] *Public financing of the social sectors in Angola*, August 2002, UNDP, IOM, UNICEF, WHO in partnership with Ministry of education, Ministry of finance, Ministry of health.
[4] United Nations Children's Fund, *The Progress of Nations 1999*, New York, 1999.

firm that in the course of these operations FAA soldiers raped and robbed the civilians that they were meant to be protecting. They conducted *batidas* – pillage operations whereby FAA soldiers looted villagers' belongings, right down to the doors and roofs of their houses, and forced the villagers to carry their own looted possessions to market or to FAA bases. During the decade from 1992 to 2002, under duress from either UNITA or the FAA, around 2.5 million people thus abandoned their homes, fields, livelihoods and communities, and crowded into the towns and cities. Initially they huddled by the thousands into decrepit buildings – abandoned railway stations and crumbling factories. They lived crammed together for years at a time in the most unsanitary conditions. Where space and security permitted they subsequently moved out of the city centres into the vast, sprawling camps of small mud huts that, by the end of the war, ringed every major city in the interior. Penned into the urban areas by UNITA attacks and FAA orders, these crowds of the internally displaced had little access to land or employment. Most of them were denied any means by which to support themselves in dignity. They received no meaningful assistance or services from the Angolan government, and survived on their own wits and ingenuity. The lucky ones were able to receive international aid. Many who found themselves in government-controlled towns, which, for strategic or security reasons were inaccessible to humanitarian agencies, starved. Everyone who could afford to escaped to the major coastal cities which were relatively untouched by the fighting. All of the stories in this book were related by those left behind in the misery of the interior.

Caala
September 2000

What do I think of this situation? It's been a long time since I thought about it at all. I am 65 years old and today my life is

2000 © Atsushi Shibuya

A malnourished child in a nutrition centre. Caala 2000.

behind me. I would like to forget what I am living through here, so that I only remember the best times. At the moment the most important thing for me is to know what will happen to my children and my grandchildren because, unlike theirs, at least my life has included moments of happiness... (Silence) I've known war, of course, but from 1958 – the year of my wedding – until 1981 my wife and I lived very well. We grew a lot of food and always had plenty to eat on our plates. I think that those moments were the only moments of peace which my children have known. From 1981 onwards the situation became very tense. Little by little UNITA's regular incursions gave rise to a climate of apprehension. That same year all of my cattle were slaughtered. I tried to build up a new herd by doing some trading, but I was knocked over by a car. It is this war which has mutilated me. Despite everything, that period was bearable. But since 1992, the situation has been quite simply unliveable.

That's why I'm here today; to escape UNITA's indiscriminate attacks because nowadays absolutely anyone is a potential target for UNITA. That's what frightens me, and what makes these attacks now different from the earlier ones because while before, UNITA were only interested in the young people who could fight for them, today they execute anyone who does not fight for them. So, children and old people – like me – are also obliged to run away. We had to leave very quickly, with no regrets. That was quite easy because at any rate all of my belongings had already been looted... (Silence) I arrived here on May 28, 1999 with my wife and my five children. We made our journey in two stages. First of all we went from Camanla into the bush, where we stayed for a few days, waiting for the road to be safe. Then from there we followed the road to Caala. I thank God for protecting us the whole way. Today I am worried because we have been told that we will soon have to return to our land. I don't really know what to think of the idea. It's true that here we live in very bad conditions, but would we be better off returning there? For me it makes no difference because I'm old, but it's different for my children and their children. They are young and would be perfect targets for UNITA, especially after having lived in a government area. We haven't yet been given a fixed date for our departure, but today everyone knows that the situation in Kuima is exactly the same as when we left. In fact, only last week there was a particularly deadly attack in a small village near to Kuima. What people say is that an informer told UNITA about the FAA's movements, so UNITA took advantage of a FAA retreat to enter the village and massacre 13 people. So I doubt that the situation is safe enough for us to be able to return. I prefer to stay here – in spite of myself – than to get myself murdered there. I've known war, my children have known war, and my grandchildren are getting to know it. I would have liked them to be able to know something else…. (Silence)

I would also have liked them not to have to know this life as a displaced person. It's a miserable life. We have nothing, and what little we are meant to receive is stolen then sold to the local people. I'm talking about the ration card of the [International Committee of the] Red Cross. I, for example, have not been given a card, even though I signed up just like everyone else on the list of the displaced. I think I'm not the only one in this situation. In fact most of the time what the local officials do is they keep the ration cards and then sell them to the local people so that those who are really in need don't get anything. In my case it's really a problem because I'm old and I'm no longer strong enough to work for the local people to earn a bit of money. And even if I could, they prefer to hire someone younger. So my life is reduced to almost nothing…. I get up in the morning and I have nothing to do and nothing to eat. At home I would get up in the morning and go to work in my fields in order to feed my whole family. Here, it is my children who support me because they work in the fields of the local people. But once the food reserves run out the situation becomes really critical…but I should not complain because at least today my family and I are alive and we can sleep more easily. Two weeks ago, my nephew went to try to work in the fields he'd left at home and he was captured by UNITA. He just wanted to fetch a bit of sweet potato because the ration from the Red Cross was not enough for all of us. (Silence) Today I have no idea what has become of him.

We were living in a neighbourhood two kilometres from the town and FAA came and advised us to leave and go to the bush. If they hadn't I surely would have died. I'm old and I can't go quickly. I left with my daughter, her husband and three children. FAA was also with us. We didn't stay long there, we could hear the gun shots and the bombs, we could see the houses burning and my daughter's husband said that we must leave. When we arrived in Matala we had nothing. We didn't bring anything with us. We stayed in a centre there for a week and registered with the government. We didn't receive any food; it was only the people who had some who shared it with us. All the people from our neighbourhood came here, so we did to.

I lived in Chipindo until 1988 when we fled from the war. We were always suffering there, we couldn't stay any longer. We went and lived in Namibe. There my husband was working as a teacher. After he died life was very difficult because it was very expensive to live there. My daughter's husband was a fisherman but he didn't earn enough for all of us, so we left and went to Dongo. In Dongo we had a field and cows. Life was almost normal. I have no sons. They all died when they were very young. I had nine, all sons, but they all died of a sickness. There was a hospital in Chipindo, it belonged to the church. I can't remember very well but it had lots of medicines and material, there was just no possibility to help my children. I just didn't have luck. The colonial times were very, very good. We stayed well and had a lot to eat. I would like it very, very much if they came back. I don't know if this war will end, I don't know these sorts of things. But we are thankful for the foreigners who have come here and who have brought us food.

Lombe
December 2000

I have a ration card. All of my people have received a card. I also have land that is part of a big field for the people of my home area. We are negotiating for another field. Still, it is not enough because of the theft. Before, the theft was FAA troops coming at night to the area with women traders from Malange, and the FAA would sell to them the manioc of our fields. This past year, it is just more general thieving. I received a distribution of five kilograms of corn seeds and one kilogram of peanuts. This is not enough, I need 15 kilograms. To earn some money, I make mats, sell charcoal, and sell tomatoes from my garden in Malange.

I come from Cuale, in the northern part of Malange Province, near Uige. In the colonial times, it was a rich area, with coffee plantations. There were several waves of departures from my village in the north. I was in the first one, around 1989. I left to go to Malange [city] because of violence, mostly by UNITA against the population. UNITA was killing *sobas*.[5] Over the years, they killed many *sobas* in my area. They killed them with knives, guns, machetes. One part of the village was burned with people in their homes. Much of this violence was because of the elections. Beforehand it was to intimidate people into voting their way and later because they blamed the people for the MPLA's victory. The [MPLA] administrator fled to Malange. UNITA was massacring areas where the MPLA was victorious. Later, I was in Malange for the first bombing. I stayed two years there, in Carreira neighbourhood. People from my home area were scattered with other people all over. I hired a house for my family and sold charcoal or collected wild fruits to get by. I also started some vegetable gardens. My wives went to the fields to get wood for the family. The situation improved with the arrival of the aid agencies. After a few

---
[5] Traditional village chiefs. Both belligerents regarded the *sobas* as threats to their authority and control over the civilian population. They were frequently targeted throughout the conflict.

years, the government resettled me from Malange to Lombe. During the last bombardment, I was in Lombe. UNITA came and killed people in Cafundanga. They destroyed the bridges during three attacks on Lombe. I fled briefly to the bush during these attacks. When I fled, FAA soldiers were fleeing in front of me. That is why UNITA was able to destroy the bridges. I would like to return to my home area. It is okay here, but there would be big problems without the [United Nations World Food Programme] food distribution, especially for the sick and the weak. There aren't many landmines in my home area, just around the towns, but not inside them.

Matala
February 2001

We fled Chipindo in 1988 because of the war. There was a big attack, like the one in Dongo, and we fled and never returned. We went to Dongo and stayed there. We didn't return to Chipindo during the years of peace because we were waiting for the elections to pass. After the elections, UNITA retook Chipindo and are still there until this time. Our troops [FAA] have tried three times to retake it but have failed and now there are many, many UNITA there. We lived in Dongo for a couple of years but when UNITA took control of Dongo after the elections, we fled to Matala but returned the following year once the government regained control. We fled from Dongo again in 1999. I grabbed one child and my wife carried one on her back and another in her arms, the others ran with us. My oldest son fled in a different direction and ended up in Jamba.[6] We only received news that he was there and still alive once we got here. Now he is here with us. When we went to the bush, we waited there for three days with FAA, to see if they would go back. Finally they called a meeting with all the

---

[6] A town in Huila Province, not UNITA's former headquarters.

people in the bush to say they weren't going back and that we must all go to Matala. Later on we heard that there were 1,800 UNITA and only 400 FAA.

We arrived in Matala and the government sent us here. Here we receive food but we don't have fields because the only land which is free, very far away, has no water. We don't have any blankets either because we left everything we had there. We want to go back but it is not safe. My brother went back but he said UNITA is still around making problems for the people who are still there. We don't want to go to [the IDP camp at] Njavei because it is not safe either. When UNITA are around Dongo they travel through that area. I have heard that there are five or six UNITA around there stealing the cows. I don't want to move there. I would rather wait here until Dongo is safe, and then go back there. I have fled many times in my life and lost everything and built another house somewhere else. Now I have a house here and I will wait here until it is safe to return, there is no point in moving to Njavei. But I am afraid to go back to Dongo because we don't know when this war will end, and even if it is safe to return for a while, we don't know what will happen next. We don't know when UNITA will come again. I don't think this will ever stop. My children went to school in Dongo. My oldest son is 17 years old. He is studying in the fourth class. The problem is that if he becomes a soldier with FAA now, he will have no education when he returns. He could be a teacher or a nurse but the only job for him here in Angola is to be a soldier. It is the only work they can do.

I was a FAPLA soldier from 1977 to 1984. I moved around all over Angola. But the war is not like it was then. It has changed. Then, when I was with FAPLA, we respected the people, now there is no respect. UNITA used to leave the people alone, now they will just kill everyone, and take the things from the people; even the FAA steals the cows from the people. Now the war is a business. In Chipindo, we had a hospital before UNITA came but when they arrived they just destroyed all the buildings, including the hospital. In Dongo there was a hospital, but it had no medicines. What is a hospital with no medicines? Nothing but a building. The government was meant to provide the medicines, but in fact you can only find these medicines in the market, where the people have to buy them. It is only the people in the cities that know these people [government officials] are thieves. The people in the villages don't know because they don't know the way that life should be. And the *soba* can't talk about things like this to the government. They are afraid and they don't have the freedom to talk about this. People think that the people in the villages are stupid; they think that we don't know, but we do. We know that the government and the FAA too, steals but we can't say anything. But we're not stupid. We know.

♀
Matala
February 2001

From 1977 to 1983 I was a soldier. I worked with the Civil Defence.[7] We trained to fight in combat. In 1983 they asked me to move to Lubango but I had five children so I didn't want to go. I didn't want to go to the town, I wanted to stay where my children could play and be free. So I had no work. But the Cubans arrived and they told me that I should look for a job with the government and I found work in a hospital with the Cubans. I was attending to the sick and dressing wounds. I worked there for seven years until the Cubans left. Everyone was very sad to see them go. My husband was also a soldier with FAPLA. He was a soldier for 13 years before he was shot and killed by UNITA in January 1991. I was there in Kuvango alone, I had no family there, only my children. The Cubans had left so I had no job either. One day the FAA came and wanted to take my clothes, food and other things. I refused to give them to them, so they began shooting at me. They shot at me 10 times. They shot at my chest eight times, but because I had been a soldier I moved like this (pretending to dodge bullets), the ninth entered my foot here and the tenth landed right there in front of my other foot.

---

[7] *Defesa Civil*: This is a civilian militia, recruited and armed by the MPLA to fight against UNITA.

After this happened, my husband's family came to get me and I went to live with them in Cambole, a small village, two days walk from Kuvango. In this place everyone was afraid of both FAA and UNITA. UNITA didn't trust the people and FAA didn't trust the people. UNITA and FAA lived a long way away, but we were in the middle. Some people were UNITA supporters and some were MPLA supporters, but we lived together, we even ate together. But I had worked for FAPLA for seven years, I was an MPLA supporter. Both the FAA and UNITA would visit us there sometimes, they would come and ask for food, but they didn't kill anyone. On March 3, 2000, I went to a meeting UNITA had with the people. I was MPLA but I just wanted to listen. They said that we must start to kill MPLA supporters, one by one, because we don't trust them. They had weapons but no courage so nothing happened.

On March 7, 2000, the FAA came to the village and took 16 or 17 people. Just women and children and one little boy...They took me and all my family, four of my children, my nieces and nephews and aunts. They took all the clothes, food, goats and chickens and made us carry them. The next morning, they gave us breakfast; a good breakfast with *funge*[8] and chicken which the women prepared. Then we began to walk again but I was behind because I could not walk very fast because of the wound in my foot from when I was shot in the foot in Kuvango and I was carrying my child on my back. I told my son that he must wait and walk with his mother. We were behind the group and I heard shooting so we hid in the long grass of a field we were passing. We stayed there listening to the shooting until it had stopped. We stayed there for a long time and then we continued along the road. We arrived, not so far away from where we were, and it was like someone had just slaughtered goats, blood everywhere and all the people lying dead, right there in the middle of the road. The FAA had just turned and open fire on the people, just like that. It was just women and children that lay dead in the middle of the road with blood everywhere. When FAA troops arrived back in Kuvango, the chief asked them what had happened there in Cambole. They told him that they had taken some people but

---

[8] A paste made from cassava flour and water - the staple in much of Angola.

then decided to kill them instead of bringing them to Kuvango. The chief was very angry and ordered the soldiers to go back and bury those people. They went and buried them along the road, but people that had since come that way say that the rain had washed the ground away and they could see the bones of the children. When I arrived in Kuvango, I was very, very angry. I went to the commander. I recognised some of those soldiers who were there and I knew who the commander was, from when I worked with the FAA in the hospital. I asked him, how could you kill my family? How could you not recognise my daughter, Victoria? How could you not recognise my children? He said that he was not there and he hadn't sent these troops to kill the people. He said that it was not his fault, but these soldiers would be punished. After this I heard that they were looking for the troops to put them in prison but until the time I left Kuvango, nothing had happened. Now, I don't know…After this attack, some people fled to the government side, here to Matala. Others stayed there. The government is our father. I worked for them for many years. I cannot stay in the bush alone to die. I would prefer to come here and die in the hands of the government.

Cuito
May 2000

Around 9 o'clock, in the morning of January 1, this year, I was bathing in a river close to Canhongo, my village, when approximately 30 FAA soldiers approached us. There were also around 10 civilians with them and the civilians were carrying stuff on their heads. As I was the only adult there, one soldier told me to get out of the water. I left the water, put on a shirt and this one soldier told me to get a basin of *bombó*[9] to carry. He was actually ordering me. The whole time when he was talking to

---

[9] Soaked and dried cassava, used to make the cassava flour which is the basis of *funge*.

me he had his AK [automatic rifle] in his hand and he used it to point at the basin, but he did not have me at gunpoint. He said I should carry it up to Chipindo, which is located four kilometres before Camacupa, and from there on other soldiers would take the things.

As we were walking I found out that they were coming from the villages of Muquinda and Missene and were actually heading to Camacupa. The civilians in the group were from these villages and they had also been required to carry the things for the soldiers. Basically they were taking things that belonged to the populations of these villages like chickens, beans and *bombó*. The soldiers were not carrying anything at all. They did not shoot at first when we were walking, but less than one kilometre later they started again. They were shooting into the ground, just to scare us, to make us feel afraid and to make us go faster. When we came close to a river, after having walked a little over one kilometre, the ground was slippery and I fell. One soldier came closer to me and said, "You don't want to carry these things, you're thinking about running away." And he shot at me, straight in my foot...and he said that it was because I didn't want to carry the things. They continued walking and left me there, hurt. The soldier who shot at me was drunk.

♀
Cuito
May 2000

We heard the shooting and the people from my village ran into the bush. Usually, when they come for a *batida*,[10] they shoot into the air in a certain way so that after a while we came to identify it, and when people heard it they ran away to avoid getting caught. It was not the first time that FAA troops had come to our village to take us for a *batida*.

---

[10] A *batida* is the name given to the practice whereby FAA troops loot villagers' possessions and force the villagers to carry them to market or to FAA bases.

2000 © Juan Carlos Tomasi

People waiting for food distribution. Matala 2000.

I don't remember how many they were, they were very numerous, certainly more than 50 but fewer than 100. I ran into the bush but I had my baby on my back and he started crying. That's how they found me. I was taken, along with a group of another 20 people, to go and collect food from the fields that belonged to the people of our village. We were taken at gunpoint. I was later given a 45 kilogram bag of maize to take up to the FAA base at Caluapanda, in Cuito. To get there I walked for two days, with the bag on my head and my baby on my back. There were other civilians and troops in my group, but others also headed in other directions. In my group there was an older man, more than 60 years old, who was given a very heavy bag to carry. Because of the weight he was always behind the group and all the time he had a soldier beating him for that. At some point he couldn't carry the bag anymore and was beaten to death. I saw a soldier hitting him hard with his feet and the barrel of the AK [47]. After that the old man couldn't walk anymore. The civilians were told to keep walking and stop looking, which we did. On the way back I saw the body of the dead man lying on the way, in the bushes. During the *batidas* they also took belongings from the people in the village like blankets or cooking utensils. If the population happens to spend the night with the soldiers during the *batidas*, they separate the men from the women. The women sleep in the same area as the soldiers and at night they rape the women.

Cuito
May 2000

During the peacetime they stopped the *batidas* but they started again last year. In 1999, there was an uncountable number of *batidas*, one after another. People had to take everything to the homes of the troops. It is mainly the low ranking soldiers who do it. People cannot refuse because they threaten you with death if you do. A few died on the way because it was too hard for them. They take people of all ages, even the elderly. They take everything they find, even clothing and household objects.

♀
Cuito
May 2000

The FAA started raping at the same time they started the *batidas*. Sometimes they do not rape the women but they make them take their clothes off so they can check if the women are carrying money on them.

♀
Cuito
May 2000

Before, the FAA did not rape women. They have started with this war. Single or married women, it doesn't matter. They break into the houses; tell the man to leave, threatening him at gunpoint, and then they rape the woman. I don't know any cases of one woman raped by many troops, but cases of women raped by one soldier I know many.

Matala
February 2001

I was born here in Tchipopia. My father is still here, I have come
to visit him. I learnt English from visiting Namibia. I have been
living the last three years in Santa Cruz [on the border with
Namibia]. Now I will go back there and get my family and take
them to Cuando Cubango. Life is okay there, almost normal.
UNITA is 40 to 50 kilometres away.

In 1976, when I was 16, I was taken by FAPLA to Cuito to
fight. This is where this happened (he said pulling up the leg of
his trousers and showing the scars from a bullet in the knee. He
was on crutches). I was sent to the hospital in Cuando Cubango.
Recently, I went to Namibia to the doctor but they asked me for
15,000 rand.[11] Where can I get money like that? I have stopped
believing there will be peace in Angola. You see, the war here in
Angola, is like a job. The people don't want this war to end.
People want to fight because this is what they know; this is what
they are used to. If you take this war away from these young boys
they will cry. This war in Angola is a business. Everyone has an
interest in this war. Even the people who sell arms, they sell them
to both sides because they benefit when the arms are destroyed
and then the armies have to build up again. And America doesn't
want this war to end – they have too many interests here. Even
the MPLA and UNITA want the war to continue. When FAA took
Jamba[12], where Savimbi was hiding, the government stopped
them. They could have destroyed it and crushed UNITA but the
government stopped them to give UNITA a chance to build up
again so they could continue to fight.

The problem is that the young people don't know the colonial
times. They have never seen how this country can be. All they
know is war. The colonial times were so good. I think it would be

---

[11] South African and Namibian currency.
[12] UNITA's former headquarters in Cuando Cubango.

good if they came back to show the youth how life here can be. There are very few people with a good education. The children don't want to become doctors and teachers; they would rather sell something to earn a couple of kwanzas[13] a day. If you tell a child that they must go to school, they will say, "OK, today I will go to school but what will I eat tonight?" The government does nothing for the people of Angola. They just take the money for the school and hospital and put it in their pockets. It doesn't matter to them because if their child is sick they just send them to Namibia or South Africa and they just send their children to school to be educated outside Angola. This is the way it is here in Angola. They just use the people to fight the war. Most of the time, people don't expect these things from the government because they don't know any other life. And even if people do, the first group that even begins to speak about these things will be punished or killed. So the people just continue to suffer because there is nothing they can do. Here, the war will only stop when all the Angolan people are dead. That is the only thing that will stop the war, when there are no more people left to fight or die.

🜨

Matala
February 2001

I am a teacher. I have been a teacher since 1969. I grew up in Huambo but when I started teaching the government sent me to Caconda. I lived there for many years and I became a member of [the MPLA's youth movement] JOTA, and was a chief of the organisation as well as a teacher for them. In 1976, UNITA was looking for me because I was a chief of JOTA so I had to flee to the bush for six months. I also had problems with FAPLA because at that time the MPLA weren't like now. At various stages of my life I worked in the schools with UNITA and the MPLA. Both had schools but the

[13] Angolan currency.

difference was that UNITA schools didn't have any materials. The children had to write on the ground or on leaves. The schools on the government side usually had materials. The other thing that was different was that the government paid salaries to the teachers, but UNITA just forced the people to work without paying them. It was obligatory. The problem was that we had to go to Lubango to receive our salaries. One day I was travelling back to Caconda, on a motorbike, with my cousin after receiving our salaries and we met UNITA. This was in Chicomba. They caught us and tied us up and the intention was to kill us. They said that we were spies, that we had new clothes and money, that we had come from the government side. When we were tied up in the village, someone passed who recognised me. He was family though I had not seen him for a long time since we were living together with the government and he had been taken by UNITA. He spoke to the chief and asked him to let us go. They took our money but let us go and we returned to Caconda where our families were.

I stayed in Caconda until 1985, and then I went to teach in Lubango. I stayed there until 1996. In the beginning life was good there but it became very expensive and difficult for my children, so I asked to be transferred to Matala. I have been teaching at the school here in Kilometre 9 since then. Life is okay here. I have a small kitchen garden here and my wife exchanges the vegetables for maize in the market. The problem is that the government doesn't always pay the teachers and they are always months behind. They never paid us for June and July for instance. The money stops in Lubango. The chief there likes to make business with this money.

Cuito
May 2000

In March [2000], the government started telling us, the civil servants, that we had to go back to rebuild the town. So we left on the morning of April 4. Around five in the afternoon, when we were close to Canjamba, only 10 kilometres from Chinguar, we were ambushed. They were too many...they were hiding in the bush and I couldn't see much. When our truck drove by them they started firing at us, ordinary AK bullets but also these little explosives that they attach to the AK.... My assistant panicked and threw himself out of the truck. In the process he pushed me out and I fell on the road, just to find several UNITA soldiers coming towards me immediately. I started running as fast as I could and they came after me. One of them was saying, "Catch him alive...it's not worth wasting ammunition on him." When they realised that despite my age I run very fast, they started shooting at me. One of the bullets hit my upper right arm and I had to have surgery.

Caala
September 2000

I left Lupili in January 1999 because of the constant massacres and thefts carried out by UNITA. We couldn't bear to live like rats any longer, so we decided to come to the government side. When we left Lupili we headed directly for Caala. We were placed in Salsicharia[14] in January 1999. I came with my wife and two of my five children. Two of the others are today fighting for UNITA because they were forcibly recruited, and I have heard that the other was murdered in March 2000. I think that they must have murdered him because they knew that I was a *soba*. The displaced people who arrived after me are the ones who told me. They saw my son being massacred and the enemy told them to come and tell me about it because they knew that I'd run away to Caala.

The life that we led in Lupili was a life of luxury compared to

---

[14] A disused factory inhabited by IDPs.

life here. But that was before UNITA started stealing everything we owned to reinforce their supplies. We used to have cattle and we grew a lot of things. But since UNITA didn't feed their soldiers they used to come into our houses and onto our land and pillage everything in their path. And if you refuse to give them your things they kill you with a machete. So it's better to give them everything. At Salsicharia there was no UNITA but the living conditions that were imposed on us by that place were almost as horrible. We used to sleep all one on top of the other and we never knew who was lying next to us because even in the middle of the day, we were living in darkness. The conditions were ideal for diseases to appear, and that's what happened. Lots of children died because of the dirty conditions we were living in.

In June I went to a meeting of the party [MPLA] where they announced that we were going to be moved to a new site. We were told that in the new site we would have the support of various aid agencies working in healthcare, food distribution and water and sanitation. When I told the IDPs from Lupili who were in Salsicharia all of this, they were very happy because at any rate we had to find a solution so that our children would stop dying. We were brought here at the beginning of August. It's true that the health situation has improved. But the problem of food, which was supposed to be resolved, has got worse. And since we're now far away from everything, it takes a lot more time to go and fetch firewood and to take it to sell in the market in Caala. Fortunately I've managed to finish building my house, but it's the only thing which is ready out of all that the government promised us. I don't know if the government made us believe in things that they already knew were not possible, or if those things are really going to materialise and it's just a matter of time. I don't know. (Silence) And then they told us that we would also have fields here, but so far there is no sign of them. We will see…. Apart from that, we haven't been able to build solid [brick] houses, like in Cantão,[15] because the water [for making the bricks] is much too far away. And anyway, making bricks takes a lot of energy, and it's difficult to find any when you're hungry!

I am tired of this war which makes us live like animals.

---

[15] Another IDP camp near Caala.

(Silence) In effect I've already lost three of my children, even if in reality only one of them is dead. But I don't have much hope for the other two. Perhaps, if God protects them…I also lost my brother and my sister in Calima in 1980. They were killed whilst trying to run away from a UNITA attack. I really wish this war would end. I am already old, but the two children I have left still have a life ahead of them. If the military situation improves I would really like to go home, to carry on cultivating my land so that my children can continue their studies to become a mechanic and a driver.

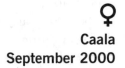

♀
Caala
September 2000

When they started burning people inside their houses, we decided to run away. That day, it was the end of December 1998, they came at five in the morning to burn the village. They did one of two things: either they killed the people first and then burnt them along with the house or they put a whole family alive inside and then they set fire to the house. Anyone who tried to escape was killed with machetes. That's how my aunt, my uncle and their son were killed. UNITA massacred them first, then put them inside the house and burned the whole lot. This is the first time that I've been forced to go far from home. But for the two months before we left Catata we had to live in the bush. In fact, throughout November and December 1998 we went every night to sleep in the bush and then went back to our houses at dawn.

　I fled with my five children. The sixth was born here. We went to Cuima on foot, then, from Cuima to Caala we travelled in FAA trucks along with eight other families. They told us that we had made a good decision in coming to them, and that they would bring us to somewhere that we could live in safety. I arrived in Caala in January 2000. My family and I were placed in [the disused factory of] Engenharia along with all the other IDPs from Catata. Life was very difficult in that place because we were all living one on top of the other. Diseases spread and the children were often sick. We had to live in those conditions until August, when we were transferred here. In fact, at the beginning of August we were informed that we would be relocated to [the IDP camp at] Cantão. The [MPLA] administrator told us that the Red Cross would come and register all of the displaced, house by house, so that everybody could have a ration card. But until today nobody has come, and we are really hungry. It's true that here we have a health post, and it's possible to treat the children, but we're really short of food. It's very difficult to live like this because we had everything that we needed in Catata. We had enough food for our own consumption, and we could even sell some to the other markets. Maize, potatoes, cassava, onions, cabbage and radishes sold the best. So you can see why it's difficult for us now to put up with these conditions.

My parents lived through the time of Portuguese colonisation. It was difficult because it was a life of slavery, but at least they weren't subjected to the trials that we're subjected to today, and they were never short of food. After independence we started fighting between ourselves, just when I thought that at last we

Displaced people living in a gym in Caala. Caala 2000.

were going to smile. Not a bit of it. This is the heritage that I leave to my children.

ʘ
Caala
September 2000

My father and my grandfather were killed the same day. It was in September 1998. They were both at home. UNITA men entered and killed them, for no reason. But I think that they killed my father because he was a *soba*... (Silence) The *sobas* are generally the first people targeted. That's part of the strategy of both UNITA and the government. Because of their status, it is them above all who inform the population of each neighbourhood if there is going to be an attack. By eliminating the *sobas* the population becomes more vulnerable and exposed to surprise attacks. So, since my father was killed, we've been sleeping with only one eye closed. We spent the six months prior to our departure going back and forth between Cuima and the bush. We spent the night there and only went home in the early morning. We spent that whole time living like that, until we had to take the decision to leave.

So, in March 1999, I brought my whole family to Caala. The IDPs who had arrived in Caala a few months earlier had sent word to us that the humanitarian organisations here would take care of us. And also, I knew Caala a bit because I came here many times to do business. We left Cuima at eight in the morning, and arrived in Caala about three in the afternoon. That was March 18, 1999. I am one of those who are lucky enough to have a ration card. Thanks to the Red Cross I receive maize flour, red beans and cooking oil every two weeks. But the quantities they give are not enough when you have to share them with several families, as in our case. For example, today we have nothing left from the distribution which was made four days ago. And it's like that every time.

Either we share, or we get robbed. And the thieves are both displaced people, and locals.

If someone had told me that one day I would be this hungry I would never have believed them. Because my fields used to give me everything I needed. I could even build up reserves to see us through the difficult times. But it's better not to think about all that because everything must have disappeared by now. Generally when an offensive makes the whole population of a village run away the bandits take advantage of the situation to move into the houses and use the fields. That must be what is happening at Cuima today. Our houses must have been occupied by those who chased us out. Here we also have a problem of blankets. There are many of us who don't have any, and at this time of year the nights are very cold.

I can't tell you how long I can put up with these conditions. In any case, that doesn't depend on me. Maybe tomorrow I won't be here any more, maybe tomorrow I will return to Cuima. That is apparently what the government is planning. According to the government there are too many of us here and the town of Caala can no longer support us. According to the government we would be better off at home, cultivating our fields. But our *soba* has advised us to refuse to return because there was fighting last week near to Cuima. First a convoy belonging to Sonangol[16] was attacked, and then a village was surrounded and burnt. All the people who tried to run away were massacred. It seems that it was people from UNITA who did all of that.

We're waiting to see what the government will decide. But that could be decided from one day to the next. As for me, I know what would be waiting for me if I go back there – certain death. What frightens me about this war is that it's getting more and more violent. It wasn't like this before. (Silence) I have the feeling that the tactics, methods and tools are changing. It's more difficult to escape from it. Before, we heard the shooting from far off which gave us the time to run away. Today, since they kill with machetes, we don't hear the noise. They knock at your door.

---

[16] The Angolan State Oil Company.

I left Cuima for the second time in 1999. The first time was in 1979 when UNITA's incursions into the town became more and more violent. We found refuge in the town of Lungo and stayed there for 12 years. It was only in 1991, after the Bicesse Accords, that it was possible for us to set foot in the town of our birth once again. We left behind the life that we had built in Lungo to return to life in Cuima. When we got home, our house was nothing more than a pile of cinders. We had to rebuild everything and clear our fields, just to leave again eight years later with nothing in our hands. (Silence) This time only my wife came with me because all of my children already have their own families and have set up their own households. They had to flee, like us, but today they are living at Cantão. My wife and I have been here since September 7, 1999. We came on foot and it took us a day and a half. When I arrived I was suffering from anaemia, but now I'm feeling better.

Life is very trying in this camp, especially at our age. Since we have no ration card we are obliged to find other ways of getting something to eat. So we get up very early in the morning to go and fetch firewood to sell on the market. That brings us a little bit of money, which allows us to buy some *bombó*. We make one meal a day from it, which is not enough, so we sleep with rumbling stomachs. We would like to do what the other IDPs do. Most of them work for local people. But because of our age none of the locals want to buy our services. I'd like to do some work as a cobbler, but I haven't got the right materials. If I had the materials I could do it because despite my age I can still remember my trade.

But it wasn't always like this. During the first three months after our arrival here, we used to go back and forth to the fields which we had left in Lungo, after our first displacement. We used to spend one week in Lungo, one week in Caala. But UNITA very quickly noticed our movements and captured the town at dawn one day. I remember that it was around four in the morning and most people were asleep. What saved my wife and I was the fact that on that day, we had got up very early to leave for Caala. When we heard the shooting we fled immediately, while the others were surprised in their sleep. They killed 49 people in that attack. From that day on, I think that was in December, we decided to stay in Caala.

We are waiting for our children to finish building our house in Cantão so that we can join them. We need to live near to them since it's them who are providing for us. As they are still young they can still offer their labour to the locals, which brings in a bit of money. Without them, my wife and I would definitely be dead by now. That's why, when the [MPLA] administrator told us that all the IDPs from Cuima would have to go home, I was very afraid because if my children go back, I will have to follow them. And going back, for us, means living yet again with the anguish of waiting to be attacked at any moment. And I don't want to live through that ever again. I am tired of this war and of the life that it forces us to lead. I would have liked my children not to have had to live through what I've seen, and to have had a peaceful life as farmers. I would have liked to be able to give them my fields so that they could look after them. That would allow them to have their own projects, for their children and grandchildren. But seeing how it's going, this isn't about to end today.

♂

Matala
February 2001

We came to Matala after the attack in Kuvango and went to live in Tchipopia [IDP camp]. After a couple of years the government came and asked us to move here to Njavei [IDP camp] where we would be given land so that we could have fields. But we were given bush that needs a lot of work. Many people were not able to plant this year, they will have to wait until next year. We need a lot of time to cut the trees and clear the land to prepare it for making fields. I came here with my people but now we are not happy here.

The problem is that we come from the town of Kuvango and we are used to living in the town. We are dirty because we don't have any clothes, but inside we are not people of the bush, we are not used to this life. Here we are in the bush, very far away from Matala town. If we go [to live] in the town we don't receive food, even though we are in the same situation. They just want us to stay out here far away from the town. My mother lives in the town, but I have to take her food otherwise she will die. And the food they give us is just enough to survive. Look (he said pointing to his bare feet) my family and I are still without shoes because if we exchange our food for shoes we won't have enough to reach the end of the month.

Here it is dangerous. We don't feel safe. Some bandits have been near here to steal our cows. Our fields are a long way from here and people are scared to go to the fields. And even if it is all right here now, if the confusion[17] starts again, the enemy will come here first because they don't have to cross the river. And there are spies. UNITA will come here to look and one day they will come back. Here at night we can't talk or light candles. If we do the Civil Defence will come and take you to the river and put you in and hold you there. Then they leave you in the bush. This has happened a number of times to my people here because they were talking at night. In Tchipopia it was different; you could have music and walk about at night. We are not used to this life; it is difficult to live like this. We need to be protected here by the police or the FAA. But really we don't need them; we just need weapons because we are all soldiers inside. We have civilian clothing but we have all been soldiers and we all know how to fight. We know how to read the signs (he took a knife and made a mark on a tree), this means that the enemy is that way, (then he crossed two sticks on the ground) and this means that there is a mine. We were all born and grew up in the war, so this is what we know. This is

---

[17] *Confusão*. This word is widely used in Angola to mean any kind of trouble, from a verbal argument between two people, to a full-blown battle.

the only thing that many people know how to do.

Water is another problem we have here. Many people are sick with diarrhoea. We have asked the government to make some wells for us, but until this time nothing has been done.

ʘ

Matala
February 2001

A big problem here is the rain, in November, December, January – no rain. It only began in February, but there isn't enough time left in this season. Once April comes, the season is over. And ploughs are another problem. We don't have ploughs, so we can only make little fields, like from here to that house [indicating a house about 25 metres away]. We received a distribution of seeds and a hoe – only a small container of corn seeds and two kilograms of beans. Later, we were given four kilograms of corn seeds. But that isn't enough for making fields. It will not even last one day of planting. If you go out in the morning, by now [pointing at 1:30 p.m. sun] it is already finished. Back in Dongo, we would use one sack for planting, which is about 50 kilograms. The government gave us fields, about 12 kilometres away. Land: we have. Rain: we don't have. It was late. Seeds: we don't have.

I fled from Dongo because of the "bandits of the bush" – UNITA. They came and were killing people. Even as they were entering my neighbourhood, *Primeiro de Maio*, they were setting houses on fire. They took everything: clothing, possessions, and then the cows and goats. It was three o'clock in the morning. I was sleeping. I was woken up by the sounds of shooting – *fway, fway, fway* – and bombs. *Bwow*. I just ran. You didn't even have time to look back into your house and see your family. Everybody just ran. Some this way, some went that way, others went that way (pointing in different directions). I ran for about three kilometres, then stopped to see if they were behind me. I could rest a little, and catch my breath. Then I started to look for my family. Everybody from the neighbourhood was on the road...it was the road to Matala. I asked around the people to find my family.

♀

**Caala
September 2000**

I left Cuima because I couldn't bear that suffering any longer. I couldn't bear the anguish that my family and I were cast into; the anguish of being massacred from one moment to the next. That constant tension, that my family and I lived at the end of 1998, when UNITA was attacking and killing everyone that had the misfortune to find themselves in their path. In the beginning we used to leave the village at night to go and hide in the bush. We did that for almost three months, up until the last attack, in December 1998, which made us run away to Caala. My two cousins and my brother-in-law were killed in that attack while they were in their houses. UNITA soldiers entered the houses to see if there were any people there, and when they saw my cousins they went out, surrounded the house, and set it on fire. (Silence) My brother-in-law was killed in same way. Unlike UNITA's other attacks, that one didn't end with them withdrawing from the village, instead they occupied it. So we were forced to leave. And that was very painful. (Silence) My family has always lived in Cuima, and it's hard to leave, after a whole life, with nothing in your hands.... Everything stayed behind there, everything. (Silence) I left on foot with my husband and my two children and I arrived here in December 1998. We headed for Caala because it was the nearest town which could guarantee us a minimum of security!

But we are paying with our lives for that security because here life is completely different (smiles ruefully). I have never been displaced before, so these living conditions are completely new for me and my family. We are totally dependent on aid, and if it's not delivered by the Red Cross, we end up with nothing at all. Nothing. If we at least had a little bit of earth to cultivate, we could help ourselves, but here we have nothing. And for us, who are basically farmers, not having fields means not having anything to eat. At home, at least, we had of piece of earth which we cultivated and we traded some produce which brought in a little money. We used to be able to come and buy a little soap, some cooking oil, some salt, a few clothes here in Caala and then resell them in Cuima. That, together with our fields, brought us enough money to live properly. Here, we have neither fields, nor work. So when there is nothing, there's really nothing – no work and no money to buy something to eat.

We considered, my husband and I, returning to Cuima from time to time to work in the fields that we left there. But it's too dangerous to return to Cuima if you're coming from a government zone. Because we lived decently there. (Silence) It was nothing like the conditions in which we are crammed together here. (Silence) Because in fact you are nothing when you are a displaced person, nothing. You have no decision making power over your own life, none at all. Today I can make no plans because I don't even know if I will be here tomorrow. If I were at home I could have planned to buy some cattle to help us with our farm work. I could have planted some sweet potato because sweet potato grows very quickly…in three months it would be ready to harvest. But here, even if we were given some seeds we wouldn't know where to plant them. I can't wait to go back home, but I have to wait a bit more, I don't know how much longer. There was a discussion, two weeks ago, about us returning to Cuima. Our *soba* came and informed us that the government was planning to "repatriate" us to Cuima. Our first reaction was joy because if the government had decided that, it must have been after investigating the situation in Cuima. Which must mean either that the situation was safe enough for us to be able to go back, or that the FAA was going to protect us in our own homes. But the week after that, Cuima was attacked again by UNITA. I hope that the government has changed its plans because I don't want to go back there in these conditions. I don't think anyone does. But it is the government that will have the last word. We will see… (Silence) So far they haven't given us the order to leave. But if everyone goes back there my family will also be obliged to go back.

What do I think about my life? (Smiles) That's simple: I'm 22 years old and I've only ever known either war, or periods of neither war nor peace. And today, I can't say if this conflict will ever end. I don't know…My mother used to tell me about the war when I was five years old, saying that perhaps I would have the chance not to know it. But today I always have war before my eyes. It would have been better if I'd never been born because not only is the war continuing, but it's getting more and more cruel. Before, if I remember rightly, when UNITA attacked they used to attack just to steal or kill maybe one or two previously identified people. Since 1998 UNITA's attacks have become more violent. They rob and kill everyone who passes before their eyes. At least if I hadn't been born, I wouldn't have known this suffering that I have in my heart. All that I can do is to ask God to make sure that no more weapons are sold to UNITA. That the international community put sanctions on the countries that sell weapons to UNITA…. That, I think, would be the only way to make this war end at last.

♂

Two brothers aged 15 and 17
Matala
February 2001

We left Kuvango and went to Jamba with our mother and father and older brother. We heard that UNITA was coming, so we left and came to Matala, and then we came here to Tchipopia.

In Kuvango life was almost normal. We both went to school and were studying in the 4th class. Our father had five cows and a field with lots of food. We were never hungry. One month before the attack UNITA was around Kuvango. They were near our field and we weren't able to go there, so we were suffering so much from hunger.

The attack was a surprise for everyone. It was a Saturday night and many people were out dancing. We knew that there was some UNITA about, but it was thought that there were just five or six people attacking people when they went to the fields, so no one was worried about them entering the town. Life went on as normal. They attacked in the night. There was lots and lots of shooting and bombs too. Only the FAA had tanks but after about four hours the FAA retreated and UNITA took the tanks and continued to bomb the people. There were lots of UNITA soldiers there, we saw many. There were 2,000 and General Bok. When we fled two of our little brothers, aged five and seven, who were running behind us were killed and another three children, two young girls and one young boy, were taken by UNITA. We haven't heard anything about them since. But they took many young boys and girls, like us, and they are still there.

(17 year old) We all fled in different directions. I fled across the river to the other side and hid in the bush. The water was up to here (pointing to his neck). I stayed in the bush alone from four in the morning until four in the afternoon when I found my family in the bush. They thought that I, too, had been killed.

(15 year old) I just ran. People were running everywhere. I couldn't see where my older brothers had gone but I turned around when I was running and saw that my two younger brothers had been shot. They were both lying on the ground. I didn't stop. I knew they were dead. I just ran; I didn't know where I was running but after that I didn't stop or look around. When I reached the bush I was alone for a while but then some people found me and showed me where my mother and father were. We stayed there waiting for the others to arrive. But only the two of us came.

♀
14-year-old orphan
Lombe
November 2000

I've been living with the Sisters[18] in Lombe for two years. My other sisters and my brother also live here. My sisters are 12 and

---

[18] An order of nuns.

10 and my brother is five. I was 10 years old when my mother died of a sickness. We four children stayed living with our aunt and father in Massango, which seemed to be peaceful. The FAA was living in the distance and I had not seen UNITA before this attack. One night, in 1998, UNITA came and attacked the town. We all fled together to the bush, where we stayed for two or three days before going to Massango. We moved on, arriving in Quitumbo where we stopped to work in the fields for food. One day my father went to the fields to work but did not come back. Me and my brother and sisters and aunt looked for him for two days and eventually found him dead, shot by UNITA. We went on to Calandula, and stayed there for a month, waiting for a lift. When we arrived in Lombe, we first lived with our aunt and my three cousins, but my aunt said that she did not have enough food for us and to stay away. It was then that we went to live with the Sisters. When I go to church I pray for the ones that are feeding us, and for God to save the dead ones.

MSF plane bringing supplies to Malange where MSF ran 5 feeding centres. Malange 2002.

"UNITA took my fields. UNITA took my clothes. Many years ago UNITA took one of my daughters. I haven't seen her since."

– Man, Malange. November 2000.

Part II
UNITA's War

Anyone who has lived through the war under UNITA control has endured in an environment utterly devoid of personal freedoms where "revolutionary discipline" was brutally enforced. They have survived a nomadic lifestyle of extraordinary hardship. And they have been subject to attack and retaliation by the government.

Civilians in UNITA areas, which for a long time included much of rural Angola, were viewed as a pool of forced labour for the party. As these testimonies repeatedly reveal, they were expected to provide food for UNITA soldiers whenever asked, and were frequently obliged to carry arms and supplies to UNITA forces in other parts of the country. These compulsory portering journeys could last as long as three months. Civilians controlled by UNITA were expected to attend public meetings about the politics of UNITA. Any attempts to resist UNITA's orders or even to disagree with anything the movement decreed were punished ferociously. In UNITA areas civilians enjoyed no freedom of expression or freedom of movement. UNITA exercised an extraordinarily tight and pervasive control over everybody living in their areas – nothing seemed to escape their attention. And UNITA patrols and roadblocks ensured that no one could leave UNITA's areas. Those who tried, and were caught, were often executed. Those who succeeded exposed any relatives left behind to reprisals. At the approach of government representatives – either the army advancing during wartime, or civilian administrators arriving during peacetime – UNITA expected all villagers under their control to retreat into the bush with them to avoid contact with the MPLA. Those villagers who stayed with UNITA subsequently spent years living in temporary settlements in the immense forests of Angola, moving on at UNITA's behest. Those who refused to stay were attacked by UNITA. Anyone suspected of having had contact with government areas was harshly punished. Many interviewees talk of being beaten and imprisoned for being in possession of salt, shoes, or medicines – commodities which were only available in government-controlled areas. Those who did manage to flee were often persecuted for having come from UNITA areas and so for having, supposedly, supported UNITA. Fear of MPLA reprisals caused many people to remain with UNITA, even when they could have escaped.

Alongside these civilians lived those who, by choice or by force, found themselves incorporated into UNITA's militarised party structures. The majority of them belonged to Angola's largest ethnic group, the Ovimbundu, who have always provided UNITA's principal support base. When the Cuban forces came to Angola after independence they conducted an offensive against the areas of central Angola where UNITA had strong support. Anyone associated with UNITA was forced to withdraw into the bush to escape these offensives. They left, imagining that they would soon be able to return home. In fact, over a quarter of a century later, most of those who still survived had yet to see their homes again. They were trapped in the bush ever since. For three or four desperate years UNITA's members lived on the run in the forests and deserts of southern and eastern Angola, pursued by the Cubans, until they managed to regroup and reorganise. UNITA gradually established a new headquarters at a place they named Jamba, in the far south-eastern corner of Angola, out of reach of the Cuban jets. At one stage UNITA ran a full parallel government out of Jamba, including Ministries of Health, Culture, Education, Agriculture and so forth. Hundreds of thousands of supporters and civilians were relocated to the Jamba area to provide logistical support for UNITA's war effort.

Men, women and children lived in the military bases established by UNITA across the country. While the men served as soldiers, the women and children built houses, grew and prepared food, and even accompanied the soldiers during attacks in order to help carry whatever they looted. During calm periods the bases could remain in one place for months or years at a time. During periods of fighting the bases could be constantly attacked and relocated. As time went by and UNITA expanded, it began systematically to kidnap civilians in order to bolster its military structures. These civilians were either people who were captured during UNITA attacks and ambushes, or were people living in UNITA-controlled villages. In one MSF survey,[19] 154 out of 197 women questioned (78 percent) had been kidnapped by UNITA. In particular, UNITA kidnapped children, both boys and girls. These children were taken away to live on the bases where they were placed in the homes of soldiers and indoctrinated by incorporation into Alvorada and JURA. When they grew up the boys became soldiers, and the girls, wives of soldiers. Most never had any contact with their families again until the end of the war. Many were taken at such a young age they did not remember their family name or home village. As one lady told us "Whoever enters the bases never leaves again."

Despite the fear and the lack of freedoms, life in UNITA areas was, by all accounts, not too bad until the final phase of the war, from 1998 onwards. UNITA had plenty of money, first from its Cold War allies, and subsequently from the sale of diamonds. It imported clothes, medicines, schoolbooks and such, and distributed them for free to those in its bases. It provided some limited services to the civilians under its control. Conditions in UNITA areas began seriously to deteriorate from 1998 onwards. First, because the United Nations sanctions imposed on the movement made it impossible for UNITA to import anything, including medicines. Those who have survived the war under UNITA control refer constantly to the absence in recent years of any industrially produced goods, especially salt, soap, clothes, shoes and medicine. People resorted to making clothes and blankets out of tree bark. Children in school had to write with charcoal on leaves. The sick were treated with leaves and boiled roots. From late 1999 onwards, UNITA was forced out of its headquarters in Bailundo and Andulo, and then out of most of its long-established

---

[19] Malange survey, 2002.

bases, by the FAA offensive. The movement was once again back in the situation of the 1970s. Hundreds of thousands of people spent the last years of the war living under the trees, walking thousands of kilometres, constantly fleeing FAA attacks. In the final months of the war, as the FAA's scorched earth tactics took effect, many, particularly the children, succumbed to starvation. One MSF survey, conducted in May 2002 with a group of 217 UNITA adults, found that in total the group had parented 939 children, of whom 387 (41 percent) had died. Out of those 668 children still alive at the beginning of the year, 116 had died of starvation and disease in the first four months of 2002. Civilians from UNITA areas report that, following the loss of Andulo and Bailundo, UNITA's treatment of the civilians under its control . became increasingly desperate, brutal and punitive.

The stories in this section have been divided into three groups: those who lived as civilians under UNITA control; those who chose, or were born into, life with UNITA; and those who were kidnapped and incorporated into UNITA's military structures. Many of the first group escaped from UNITA areas, or were forcibly displaced by the FAA, while the war was still ongoing. However, due to the brutal control which UNITA exercised over those in its bases, and the desperate conditions in which these people lived for the final years of the war, it was impossible to talk to either of the other two groups until the war ended. Following the cease-fire around half a million former inhabitants of UNITA's bases emerged from the bush, many of them for the first time in a quarter of a century. Malnourished and emaciated they assembled in 38 demobilisation camps across the country to await permission finally to return to their homes and families. Due to a delay in getting assistance to these camps, many more of them starved to death unnecessarily, after the cease-fire. Many of these interviews were conducted with the inhabitants of the demobilisation camps.

UNITA's Civilians

♂

Matala
February 2001

Here, the government gave us some land for all of the people but it is not very big. They gave us four cows also, but we don't have the equipment to plough the fields. When we arrived in Matala the government sent us to Njavei, but we only stayed there a few days. After that, they moved us here. They told us it was because they did not have enough food for us there and we should start a new neighbourhood here. I am from Matala. I went with my family to Chipindo in the year of peace to find some land so that we could have fields. After a short time there, the peace finished and UNITA came there. We lived there with UNITA from then until we left in January this year.

You see, it's like this: when you live there with UNITA, you must obey them. You must do what they say, otherwise they will kill you. They control the people. Even if you have the idea to go to the government side, they threaten you that if you leave they will kill you, so the people just stay there and obey them. The people can't laugh and be free to do things. If they see you laughing, they say, "Why are you laughing? Have you heard that there is peace, have you been talking with people from the MPLA side?" UNITA likes to see the people suffering, they make the people work like slaves and take the food from the people so that they are hungry. They take the children away from their parents and take them to their bases so they can work for them, transporting things and making them do anything they say. They are just like their slaves. This is why they don't want the people to go to the government side because then they would not have anyone to work for them. Once the children are about 14, UNITA starts training the boys to fight and the girls are made to dance and sing, it is called JURA. These girls must also serve the soldiers when they want. Later on these girls become their wives. These girls appear happy in the face but in their heart they are not. My sister became the wife of a UNITA solider. She, too, was taken away when she was a young girl. She was allowed to come back to the village to get food, but she did not talk about life there, no one does because they are afraid. Even to their own family, they can't talk badly about their life there because you can't trust anyone. You don't know who will tell UNITA.

I was never taken because I was a teacher of the Bible. UNITA let us have a church but we weren't allowed to sing, only talk. UNITA doesn't have churches because they don't want to bring the law of the church to their bases. The church says "You will not kill." One day UNITA came into our church and took all the young girls. They began firing bullets at the people because they were angry that they had been hiding and were not giving them the young girls for JURA. In our village we didn't have any school. Our children don't know how to read or write. They only speak Umbundu[20] because if you speak Portuguese, they say you have been with the MPLA. You must only speak with them in Umbundu. We didn't have a hospital or medicines there either. We just used traditional treatments. No, I will never go back. I would rather exchange my house for a kilo of maize than go back there.

[20] The language of the Ovimbundu people. The Ovimbundu, Angola's largest ethnic group, originate from the central provinces of Benguela, Huambo and Bié. They provided UNITA's main support base. Jonas Savimbi was Ovimbundu. However, despite this, ethnic differences have never been the motivation for Angola's conflict.

I arrived in Cangandala in beginning of October. I registered with WFP[21] and I've received one distribution of food, and seeds for planting maize. I was given communal land by the *soba* of the neighbourhood. Right now, I'm living in a small grass hut with my children and other family members. I left Mussende town in August, with my mother, brother, sister and brother-in-law, and children. My husband left in 1990. We came by foot along the road and stopped in [the village of] Kilometre 25 for three weeks to earn maize because we heard that there was no food in Cangandala.

In 1983 I left Mussende because of the suffering from UNITA and went to Kimbamba. In 1991, the government told the people there was peace and to return to their original areas. When I arrived back in Mussende there was no peace, but I could not return to the Malange area. We were not allowed to leave by UNITA. From 1992 until September 2000 we lived under UNITA. During this time there was a lot of suffering. We were forced to give UNITA food, 50 kilograms of maize per month if you were single and 100 kilograms a month if you were married. I was also forced to work in the fields, prepare maize flour and carry UNITA's arms and food for up to one or two weeks at a time.

It didn't matter if you were sick, they didn't care, you just had to continue until you collapsed, and then they would beat you, sometimes they even killed people. You would have to carry your own food, plate, water container, and children if they were still on your back. Even if you were carrying food for UNITA and you had no more, you did not touch it, otherwise they would kill you. I did not have to be a 'wife' to the soldiers, I was too old. It was only the young girls of about 15 years old. In September, 1999 UNITA

---

[21] The UN's World Food Programme.

took the whole village into the bush to live, and there the suffering was even worse. We didn't have anything. No clothes, no blankets, no salt, no medicines. We would pound the bark of the trees to make blankets. Four of my children died of a sickness, swollen feet, face and stomach, during this time in the bush because we had no salt.[22] There was nothing I could do.

**Malange
December 2000**

We come from Caxinga, but there is no one living in the town anymore. We've been living in the bush for the past year, in small groups of five or six people, all within a couple of hours walk from the town. We would sneak into town to fetch food from the fields but if you got caught UNITA would kill you. Living like that, we ate two meals a day of cassava, *funge* and sometimes fish. We got a kind of 'salt' from the river bed. We did not leave to Malange before because UNITA controlled all the paths. When the FAA came in September 1999, some people left, but others were too afraid. There are still some people remaining there living in the bush. When we were living in the town of Caxinga, before we fled to the bush, UNITA would come often and ask the *soba* for goats, chickens and other food. If the *soba* could not give it to them he was beaten. He would have to lie down on the ground like this, and two people would beat him with pieces of wood, 100 times each.

UNITA would come and take the young boys and girls. The first time they took 15, then 10 and then three. One time they took a group of children and the FAA went after them and the children escaped. The girls are taken to carry the babies of UNITA, fetch water and cook for them. The boys are taken to collect firewood, carry UNITA's food and weapons and are trained to

---

[22] This lady is describing the symptoms of oedema, a condition resulting from protein deficiency, which has been very common in Angola, and which has caused the death of thousands of children.

become UNITA soldiers. UNITA would come and make the older people carry things for them, sometimes 30 days, 15 or seven, it just depended. I was beaten three times by UNITA for refusing to carry things. I could not, the things were too heavy, but they beat me for that, they beat me because I did not do want they ordered. UNITA would come to the village every week and select the women to prepare the *bombó* and bring it to their base. Sometimes they would take the clothes of the women too. We were not allowed to use shoes. They told us shoes are only for UNITA, not for us.

Matala
February 2001

We all used to work very hard. We had cows and fields, so when all that had gone, we came here. Bandits took all of my cows, I didn't know who but when I came here I recognised some. UNITA is around the fields there so I was afraid to go. In the end there was nothing left, no reason to stay. We left because we were suffering too much. For the last year we have been going to the bush to sleep. Every night with my wife and children, just on the ground. During the day we would go back to the village but we were all afraid. Everyone was afraid to go to the fields. So I took my family and we left. We came through the bush for three days, we were slow because of the children and we only travelled at night. We couldn't walk during the day because UNITA has spies in the bush and if you are caught they will kill you and all your family.

There we were suffering. UNITA would come to our village often and take our food. Because of this we were hungry. Sometimes they would come and take the children, they would make them carry all the things they had taken and the children would never come back. We had no clothes, soap, or salt. If UNITA found that you had salt in your house they would kill you.

There, there was no school for the children to learn. Our children only speak Umbundu, they can't even speak Portuguese and they can't read or write. And no, there were no hospitals, no medicines. We just used traditional medicines, roots and plants.

Sometimes UNITA would have meetings with the people, maybe two or three days every one or two months. You had to go, everyone in the village had to, if you didn't they didn't trust you. They told us: "We must stay together and be unified, that is the message that our chief, Savimbi, tells us. That we must trust that the war is soon coming to an end and soon there will be peace. That is what we are fighting for. We will win this war very soon." In the beginning when they were telling us, I believed what they told us. I trusted what they said. But after some time I stopped believing, I lost faith in what they said. They just lied to us, but you could not let them know you thought that. If there was peace I would go back. Our land is good there; we can grow a lot of food. Here we were given land but it is under the water and the seed will not grow now. We have a ration card to receive food, but now we have to wait again until next month. Here there is a school but it hasn't started yet. There is no health post here; we have to go the hospital in Quipungo. It takes about half a day to go there by foot, but when someone is sick it takes longer.

♀
Matala
February 2001

I was born and grew up in Matala. I moved to a village in Chipindo in 1996 because my uncle was living there. My husband in Matala was beating me because he said I was going with other men. He was insane, so I left him and went to live with my uncle. I left there because we were suffering. We slept in the bush every night. Just on the ground without any blanket and it was raining a lot. We slept in different places and we had to take off our shoes because if UNITA saw the footprints they would say that you had a son on the side of the MPLA. We had to hide our shoes because they would kill you if they saw that you had shoes.

Life was difficult for me there because I didn't want to marry with a man from UNITA, so they said that I had a husband in the FAA and he was coming here to make love with me and this is why the FAA came here to attack them. They didn't trust me, so they took me to prison and I stayed there for two months. The prison was in a house, it was a hole in the ground covered with wood and then with soil on top. It was very small and we were crouched like this (she sat down bent over). It was dark. There were three girls in there also. They were there because their husbands were UNITA soldiers but they had fled. UNITA was punishing the wives because they thought they knew something about their husbands escaping. They were there when I arrived but I don't know how long they'd been there because we didn't talk. If UNITA caught us talking they would say that we were making a plan to escape. Our families would bring us food and water but they had to give it to a girl of UNITA and then she would bring it to us. During this time, my youngest child was with me but my other children stayed with my uncle in the village.

MSF doctor examining a child. Caala 2001.

2001 © Thomas Roy

On March 17, 1999 they set me free and I fled to another village, but it was still controlled by UNITA. The UNITA from the other village found out where I was and sent a letter to the *soba* to tell him to keep me there. One day an old man came and had sex with me and he became my husband. I stayed there for eight months. We planned to escape and go to the government side, but UNITA found out and took my husband and put him in prison. I fled without him, with my children and a group of people. We fled through the bush at night and it took three days. My husband was a farmer there. He had always lived with UNITA. But it was different before, UNITA was different with their people. Now UNITA doesn't forgive the people that were born there, they threaten them and kill them, just like the people who come from the side of the MPLA. When I arrived I went to Cajangite to stay with my father but I had problems there with the men, so I left and went to [the Social Affairs Ministry] MINARS. They sent us to Njavei and then after a few days they sent us here. MINARS said that there were too many people there and that we must make our own village here. Here they gave me a tent to live in with my children. I have a card to receive food. I have received food once in January.

♀
Matala
February 2001

My husband went to Matala to find some salt and other things. When he returned UNITA knew that he had gone to the government side and they captured him and put him in prison. After one day there he escaped, so UNITA came looking for me. I was in the village where we lived. They knew who I was, so they came and found me, tied my hands and took me to their base in the bush. At the time I was carrying my child on my back, but they took him away from me when they put me in prison. The prison was a hole in the ground, covered with wood and then covered in soil. They untied my hands and pushed me into the hole. It was dark and there were many other people also there. In the beginning I didn't know how many but I think there were about 20. I stayed there for about two weeks. Some people had been there for a long time, more than a month. They gave us food and water but just enough to survive and they didn't care if you died or not. We weren't allowed to talk. We just sat there in the darkness waiting to see what would happen. Some people were taken out and taken down to the river and killed.

After two weeks, they took me, another woman and two men, and sent us to another prison in Chicomba town. They tied the hands of the two men but not mine or the other woman's. When we arrived, before they put us in the prison, I escaped. I don't know what happened to the others, I escaped alone. I fled into the bush. I stayed in the bush and continued through the bush until I reached a place near our village. Here I found my husband and other people hiding in the bush. We fled in a group to Matala. Not long afterwards my grandmother came with other people from our village, and brought our children. After three weeks UNITA sent my child they had taken from me at the base to my grandmother. They knew my family well; we had always lived there in the village.

I lived in that village all my life with UNITA. I went to Matala in the years of peace but returned because we thought that there would be peace forever. This was the first time I had had problems with UNITA. I always obeyed them. When I was a young girl, they took me and another girl to their base. I stayed there for some time, until I escaped and went back to our village and married. During this time we had to dance and sing for them. They took us when they wanted to for sex. You couldn't refuse otherwise they would kill you. But they took us by force, we had no choice. My husband was a teacher and therefore he was not taken to be a soldier. There was a school but there were no materials. We had fields with lots of food but we were always hungry because UNITA would always come and take it. UNITA would have meetings with the people, you had to go – it was not voluntary. They told us that we must never think about going to the MPLA. They told us many lies.

I am happy here. All my family is here and we have salt and other things we never had living there. We have some land and we were given seeds but now the land is covered in water and the seeds have been washed away.

♀
Cuito
May 2000

At the time, in the beginning of September [1999], Camacupa was under the control of UNITA. I had saved a bit of sea salt from the times of the government. UNITA did not allow anyone to sell sea salt in the market because that was a sign that the person had had a contact with people who live in the government areas or had gone there. I was not aware of that at all. So, one day I was selling salt in the market and two UNITA came to ask me my name.... That same night, after dinner, two UNITA soldiers came to my home.... They took me to their base in town. There, they put me in jail with no justification. In jail, there were another two women. The next morning, two commanders came to interrogate me...then they gave a paper of approximately 20 cm long folded all the way and told me to keep it in my hand but not read it. I was taken back to the room. The two other women had also received a sheet of paper each.

Later on, another two soldiers came to get the papers from us and took us three to a dark room. Each one of us was whipped 50 times. Later that day, another two soldiers came and took us to an area, an open field, where a fire was lit. The soldiers were then asking themselves if they should shoot us dead or not and one replied that it would be a waste of ammunition, that they should just burn us alive. They immediately grabbed the other women and threw them in the fire. They burnt their heads, hair and one side of the face, as far as I could see it. Then they did the same thing to me. They grabbed me from behind and threw me in the fire, saying that I could not scream.

This woman lost part of two fingers, the mobility of all fingers in one hand and the mobility of one arm. Her chest and face were also badly burnt.

**Cuito
May 2000**

After the situation started to settle down, people started telling on each other. UNITA was mainly after the *sobas* but also people who worked for the government or had family members in government held areas. And these people started to disappear at night. It happened to my neighbour, his wife and his son. His son used to sell medicine in the market. UNITA must have presumed that the drugs were bought in government areas and they were all taken, in March 1999. We never saw or heard about this family again.... A lot of people died that way; all of the *sobas* from Kwanza Commune who were not in favour of UNITA were murdered. The *regedor*[23] of Kwanza Commune, Mr. Muhala, went to live with a daughter in Camacupa after UNITA came in. UNITA found out where he was, went after him and shot him dead in a neighbourhood of town. Another man, Liginda, a *soba* from Kwanza and the assistant to the *regedor*, was also murdered. His son had been in the Civil Defence forces. The *sobas* were found because one of them, one that was chosen by UNITA, told on all the others. This man, being from there, knew who the *sobas* were and where they had gone to. UNITA also finds out a lot of things by asking the children. They find a lot of people like that.

---

[23] Chief of the *sobas*.

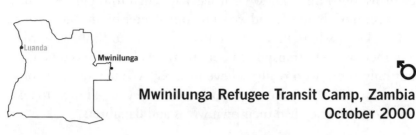

Mwinilunga Refugee Transit Camp, Zambia
October 2000

Everyone is here.

Life was made of suffering. We had a small piece of land which we cultivated, we grew cassava, sweet potato, vegetables, black beans, maize, a bit of everything, you know. But UNITA controlled the harvest. They left a bit for us, and took the rest for them. It was UNITA who controlled everybody. They used to take the men when they needed to transport weapons or other things, some-times far away, for more than three months. We used to manage by dealing with Zambia. We used to fish and hunt and then go and sell the fish and the meat in Zambia, and we would come back with soap, salt and clothes. But even then, when we went to sell in Zambia, we had to pay a tax to UNITA. We were not allowed to go to a government area, those who tried were killed. No, I didn't hear about it, I saw it. With UNITA you don't hear about things, you see them, you see deaths. We suffered a lot, a lot.

I left my village last week. It started on 15 September, UNITA told us that the war was coming, that there were battles in Cavungo and they were going to fight. And that Sunday we heard bombardments from seven in the morning to three in the after-noon. There was a lot of fighting in Cavungo, and then UNITA told us to leave. They told us that they didn't want us to stay there to listen to the propaganda of the MPLA, we, who had always lived with them. They preferred us to leave, or be killed by them, than have us fall into the hands of the government. They beat those who protested, so we left, carrying what we could.

Normally it takes four days to walk to Jimbe, but with the chil-dren we took seven days. We walked during the day and slept at night. Some went to [the Democratic Republic of] Congo, but the Congolese soldiers said that we were UNITA soldiers and would-n't let us pass. Some managed to pass anyway, saying they were civilians, but I don't know what has happened to them. We came in a group of about 50, and we were joined later by another group, I don't know where they'd come from. We got to Jimbe yesterday and then we were transported here by truck. Some stayed behind, but only those who really believe in UNITA. They did not force us to stay. Now they are in the forest. No, they didn't used to take our women. They had their own wives and daughters.

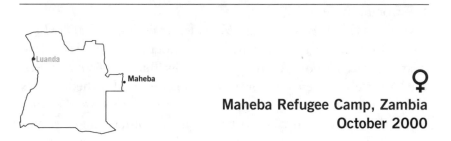

♀

Maheba Refugee Camp, Zambia
October 2000

I come from Cavungo. In 1982, I did a health promoters' course in Cazombo, then I started work in the hospital. But the hospital closed a year ago, and there hasn't been any medicine for three years. Until 1997 we were paid a salary by the United Nations. Since 1997 I haven't been working. I went back to join my husband in Cavungo. He's a teacher and is in the same position, he hasn't worked since 1997. We had some land where we planted a bit of everything, and we made *caxi*.²⁴ Besides our land there were also UNITA fields where we were obliged to work for them. We suffered from hunger. And we couldn't sleep at home because of the war, even with the rain. When the MPLA soldiers came we fled into the forest. In 1999, groups of MPLA soldiers came from time to time. They took our food and went away again. It was only in September [2000] that there was real war, and we really suffered. From July of this year we had to hide in the forest. It was the first time.

My last child was born at home, I suffered a lot. The others were born in the hospital. Luckily they've never had a contagious disease, just coughs and fevers. The last vaccination campaign was in 1998. There were schools until 1999. There were parties sometimes, for the circumcisions and the weddings, but never in my

---

²⁴ An alcoholic drink made from maize and sweet potato.

house; we didn't have the means. We didn't have to do forced labour, except for working in UNITA's fields. But they used to take the young people to carry food to the frontlines, and to train them to fight – those who didn't want to, already ran away to Zambia a long time ago. I left Cavungo in August to go and hide in the forest. The FAA arrived in August, in small groups they would come and steal all of our things, beat the people and then go away again. They stole all my clothes, my goats, my chickens, and they beat my father because he had nothing to give them. They said, "You have hidden all of your belongings," and they hit him.

In September the FAA took Cazombo and then arrived in our area. UNITA ran away, there was no fighting. When the FAA arrived my husband had gone into the forest to hunt and I had to run away on my own, with my children and my mother because he wasn't there. I left with a big group from Cavungo. We went into the forest and walked to Lovua, where there were still people. Then we walked to Luau Mission, it took a week. I ate nothing for a week. We already knew of Maheba refugee camp, but when we fled we didn't think, we just wanted to run to Zambia, to run from the war. When we got to Luau Mission we were given some maize flour, some beans, some oil and some salt. I stayed a week in Mwinilunga [refugee transit camp] where I received some more food. I got here yesterday, Thursday. Now I really want to stay here. Only if perhaps I hear that my father is still alive, then I'll go and fetch him and come back here. My father stayed behind because he can't walk. It was just suffering. I have nothing else to say. Just suffering.

🌍

Maheba Refugee Camp, Zambia
October 2000

We had nothing to eat. We suffered a lot. We had to give all of our agricultural produce to UNITA, and they left us just a little so that we would be able to continue working for them. It's been like that since 1985, they would take the food and we were even forced to carry it to the front lines for the soldiers. They would take the youngsters and force them to carry the food. Sometimes they took them away for a whole month. The women were married by force, regardless of their age. And there was no school, no hospital, no doctor, so we treated ourselves with traditional remedies. There wasn't even a nurse. No, there were never any parties, not even for the marriages.

There was fighting and bombardments. That started in July of this year, until September, when we fled. We left Lovua on July 28. We went and hid in the forest, we were camping in the forest. Then we slept four nights in the forest on the way, and we got to Luau Mission on September 16. The truck came to fetch us a week later and took us straight to Maheba, we didn't pass through Mwinilunga. We were the third group to arrive in Luau Mission. We never left before because UNITA wouldn't let us. It was forbidden. Anyone who tried to leave for Zambia was killed. We were like slaves, surrounded, we had no right to go to Luena or Zambia, we were stuck, prisoners. Myself, I was never beaten, but the young people who were forced to carry things for UNITA suffered a lot. Yes, it's true, the soldiers would take the girls that they wanted, take them away and rape them.

No, I don't think I will go back to Angola – only when there is real peace. Otherwise I will stay here forever. This is the second time that I've been here. Already in 1986 I fled to Zambia and lived in Maheba from 1986 to 1992. In 1992, when there was peace, we were taken back by aeroplane from here to Cazombo. We should never have gone back, we should have stayed here. Now we have to start all over again.

♀
Matala
February 2001

All my children, except this one, are with my husband. I have been here since January 2001. I was taken by the FAA, with five other women, when we were in the fields in our village. Someone told me that my husband was at [an office of the Social Affairs Ministry] MINARS with my children, and I went to visit them two days ago. My children are sick, they have swollen bodies;[25] I need to go and be with them and take them food. They receive food there but it is not good, it is not good for them to eat it. The problem is that I can't go there because my identification papers say that I must stay in this camp.

When the FAA found us, we were taking cassava from the fields. They said to us: "What are you doing here? Let's go. If we leave you here you will eat all the cassava," and they laughed. At night we were tied up to a tree by our feet and hands. During the day when we were walking they untied us but always walked along beside us with their guns. Even if we wanted to go pee they would come with us to make sure that we wouldn't run away. Every time the FAA came to the village I would run away. This was the first time I was caught by them. One time my husband was caught by them. He stayed with them just for the day and escaped that night. He still had his hands tied but he met someone on the way home and they untied his hands.

The FAA would come to the village and look for cows. When they knew where they were they would return and take the cows. Sometimes they would kill people, it just depended on luck. Sometimes they killed whole families and other times they would just catch someone and ask for information about where the cows were and then let them go. One day five or six FAA came to take the cows. I was in the church and they came in and started shooting. They did not kill anyone, it was just luck. In the village there

---

[25] A symptom of acute malnutrition resulting from protein deficiency.

was one school. There was no hospital, only UNITA had medicines but not for the people. There was no market. UNITA did not allow it. We had no salt, clothes or soap. When I arrived in Matala I was sent here by MINARS because this is where all the people for Chicomba are sent. I have a ration card, but I have no cooking pot.

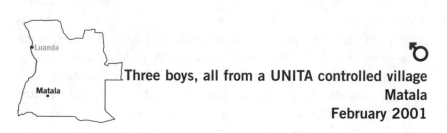

Three boys, all from a UNITA controlled village
Matala
February 2001

Boy, 13.
I came here with my mother and father and sister. My two older sisters and little brother died there of a sickness. I went to school there. We wrote on pieces of wood with charcoal. We played football sometimes but not with a ball, just a ball we made with a sock and other things. I remember a long time ago we had salt but then during this time we never had any. I remember one day at sunrise the FAA came and we went to the other side of the river and then we went back to the village in the afternoon. They took all my father's cows.

Boy, 10.
I came here with all of my family in 1999 – my mother and father and three sisters. I went to school there. We had one blackboard and we would write on it one by one. We only spoke in Umbundu, the teacher taught us in Umbundu. Sometimes we would play but sometimes they [UNITA] would not allow us to play, sometimes they would beat you. We did not play with the sons of UNITA. They would stay in the base and we would stay in the village. I remember that UNITA took our clothes and cows. I like both places but here no one bothers the people.

Boy, 10.
My family has gone to the fields to find work to get some food.

We came here three months ago, just my mother and two little sisters. My father died a long time ago of a sickness. We came with the FAA; they caught us and brought us here. They made us walk together and they walked with us with their guns. I went to school there, but it was just a school of the church. We didn't learn things like here, we just listened and sometimes we sang.

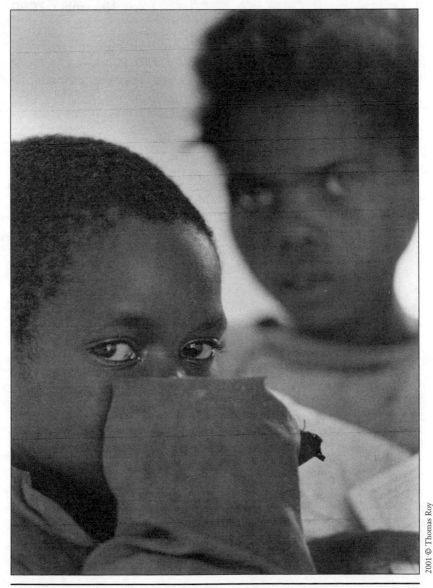

Nutritional centre in Caala. Caala 2001.

2001 © Thomas Roy

⚦

Two boys, cousins, aged 12 and 13
Malange
November 2000

About a year ago, we fled with our families from [the village of]
Kilometre 25 because of UNITA attacks. We fled into the bush,
where we lived for a year. After that, we finally reached Mussende.
During our time in the bush, one of our little brothers was lost.
He was taken by the witches.

We lived in Mussende for about three weeks. When UNITA
attacked we hid in small mud brick shelters, until the FAA chased
UNITA away. Lots of people were killed by shooting and some
people were taken alive to the UNITA bases in the bushes. Some
young women and children were taken to Caluxinga, a village
beyond Mussende. Some of the old women in the town are the
mothers of the UNITA soldiers and they tell their sons which people in the town should be killed. A lot of people were dying of a
sickness in the town, sometimes 10 a day. There are people with
swollen feet and swollen stomachs, and diarrhoea. Most of those
people were not able to leave because they were too sick. Our
brother [who was being treated for oedema in an MSF
Therapeutic Feeding Centre] also had this sickness.

There is no health post in Mussende. There is no school.
There was a lot of food in the fields, but if the people went there
they would be taken or killed by UNITA. People are not allowed
to leave Mussende, there are UNITA checkpoints everywhere. It
depends on luck [if people escape], God has to help them. Our
father sent a letter to relatives in Malange, who told us to come,
as life was better in Malange. We escaped with him and with our
sick brother, going through the bush to the River Cuanza. It took
us two days. From there we came by car to Malange. The rest of
our family will also try to come to Malange.

UNITA by Conviction

In fact I'd already been imprisoned once in May 1976. I'd gone to do the shopping and I was arrested by the MPLA, for no reason, just because I came from a UNITA area, and they said that I was a member of UNITA. But I was freed after one day by the testimonies of people who knew me. In October 1976, I was imprisoned for a second time. UNITA had gone into the bush; it was the MPLA who were in control of the region. I was imprisoned in the jail of Bié. They didn't mistreat me; it was just that the food was bad. We were four prisoners and we suffered. Then I went back home. All of my children were already born by then. They lived with me and they went to school. I stayed for another six months, and then a friend warned me that they were going to come and lock me up again, and so I left, on February 11, 1977. I hid in the forest with all of my family. We just took some clothes, some tools and our money. I hid in the forest where we joined up with some others in small villages. I started to teach my children in the forest. We went all the way to Mavinga. From 1977 until 1979 I walked, for two years. I bought food, or exchanged it for my clothes. And so, in 1979, we got to Mavinga where we stayed until 1992. It was an area controlled by UNITA and there was a school there.

In 1992, after the peace accords, I went back to Huambo. One of my sons is a UNITA soldier. Now he's in Luanda, in the FAA.[26] In Huambo in 1992 I became a farmer again. I stayed there until 1994, when I was transferred to Mungo. It was there that I was separated from my other children, now there are only two who are here with me. In 1994, the war resumed in Huambo city itself, they were bombing day and night and my house was destroyed by the bombs. In 1993, there was only a little war, some artillery fire but no bombardments. So, in 1994, I fled to Mungo. My sons were UNITA soldiers. Two had gone to Luanda at the time when the peace accords were signed; the others remained in UNITA zones as soldiers. I haven't had any news of them since then, none at all. In Mungo I went to the church and to my fields, and I lived like that until 1999. There wasn't really much war. I had a good rest. The aeroplanes didn't come as far as there.

Then, on September 21, 1999, a bomb fell on my house. I had to abandon the house and run to a village in the forest. It wasn't very far away. And there, the journey began, and the suffering. I stayed a couple of weeks near Mungo, and after three weeks the war arrived there also, so we set off again towards Andulo. I reached Andulo in the morning, and that afternoon they started bombarding. Afterwards the [FAA] troops arrived and we began the long march on September 18, 1999.

We went to a village and we decided that we'd stay there a month to rest, but after one week, at night, there was more bombing. So we set off again. We stopped somewhere in another village for a week, in spite of the bombs. Then we set off again, at random, running from the bombs which were always behind us. We walked and walked, to the right, to the left, always in the bush. We passed villages empty of people, sometimes we passed people who told us, "Don't go that way, go this way." On the way five children and two old people died of fatigue and illness. We carried three old people on our shoulders. The group was big. We didn't meet any soldiers from UNITA.

---

[26] With each peace process a certain number of UNITA soldiers were integrated into the FAA.

Eventually we realised that we were close to Zambia, so we decided to continue in that direction to find some peace and quiet. During that whole time we slept in all of our clothes, afraid that we would have to flee at top speed without being able to take anything with us. I even kept my tie on.

We arrived in Zambezi [in Zambia] in August [2000], where we stayed one week. Then we were transported to Maheba by the UN to Road 44. There we had some problems. The other refugees would not accept us, and we were transferred here, to the transit centre of Road 22. During our flight we swapped our belongings in order to eat – clothes, tools. We also found fields which had been abandoned by others who had fled in front of us. We could not head in the other direction because we were constantly running from the bullets. There was no way to evade the attacks – they wanted to exterminate us.

♀

Maheba Refugee Camp, Zambia
October 2000

I was born, I went to school, and I got married in my village. I had my children there. The war started and I lost my husband who was a nurse. He went away to work and he was killed by the MPLA in the Calai area.

I left Lobito in 1976, in the time of the Cubans. I have spent my life running away. I survived by trading with the people. From Lobito we went to the Calai region, which is where my husband was killed. Then I fled to Camundo. But we were always being bombarded. In 1990, in Licua, I was hit by some shell fragments. I was treated in the hospital of Cacuxi, on the border with Namibia. I stayed 90 days in the hospital. There were doctors and drugs. I left my married daughters there and went on to Jamea.

I started teaching in 1997 in Andulo, where I stayed from 1995 until 1999. We were bombed there all the time. War leaves people poor. We had to live from one day to the next. From 1976 until today I have done nothing but walk, and run away. I wanted to stay in Angola, that's why I never left before. But now it's too much, the bombs were even falling on the bunkers, many people died. So, I wanted to breathe a little, get out of the war, I've been too much time in the war. I lost contact with my children in July. We were attacked by the bombs and we all ran in different directions, without thinking. Since then I've never seen them again.

As far as illness is concerned, I have malaria and high blood pressure. There were no medicines there. Those who know the roots teach the others [how to treat people with them]. One of my daughters had scabies. I educated my children at home, and occasionally they would go to school. One is an agricultural engineer, the other works in computers. In 1999, I ran away from Andulo, at the end of the year, because there were too many bombs and battles. I fled with the others, with this group which is here, straight into the forest without taking anything. We were in the middle of the bullets. I don't know how I'm still alive. And it carried on like that for 11 months, until we arrived in Zambezi [Zambia]. We never stopped for more than a week, every time there was shooting, bombardments. They bombarded everywhere they saw smoke or wherever they saw crops. We came across other people, and UNITA soldiers who told us, "Go this way, don't go that way." We passed through empty villages, the people had already run away, or else they fled with us when we arrived. We suffered a lot.

Two women gave birth on the way. One had twins in May – they're fine, they're here. The other had her baby one night after we'd run the whole day. In the morning the men had to carry her on a sort of stretcher for two days so that she could get some rest. Another woman had a still-born baby. That is my story – a life of war and running away ever since 1976. Now I want to carry on working in education. Here, I can help our children. If one day there is peace again in my country, if all goes well, then I would go back there. I have lots of friends and acquaintances there, it's our land. I would go anywhere – Bailundo, Andulo, Huambo… Since 1976 I've done nothing but walk and run away.

I was born in a village and there I attended primary school. Then I went to Huambo to do secondary school, and on to Luanda to do a nursing course. After that I lived in Benguela where I worked in the hospital until 1975. When the confusion started I went back to Andulo. I looked after my house and cultivated our land. One of my daughters died in childbirth, another of sickness, of cancer.

In Andulo I worked the land and planted everything I needed. I should have worked as a nurse but there were no medicines. In Andulo, since 1975, we have not had a calm life; we had to go constantly into the bush or to surrounding villages. They were bombing wherever there was smoke or where there were fields. Between 1975 and 1992 I returned to Andulo from time to time, but we always had to go and hide in the forest again to escape the bombing and the attacks. In 1992 or 1993, it was more or less calm, but in 1993 everyone had to run away.

Since 1994 no one could stay in town, everyone was running away to the villages all the time. On October 24, 1999, I had to leave home. I left everything behind. I had some very good, very well irrigated land, some goats, pigs and chickens. I left all of that, I took nothing with me. The infantry, the tanks, were advancing towards us. The MIGs were up above, the tanks down below, I had to flee in the middle of the shooting, the bullets were whistling by everywhere. Those who died are dead. I ran away with my wife and one grandson. I found the others again on the way and I brought them with me. We left with nothing, nothing at all. Afterwards we picked up things in the villages which other people had already abandoned – cooking implements, food, clothes. And then we exchanged them for food. I had two pairs of shoes. I exchanged a much nicer pair than these for a plate of cassava. Now I have only these left. This shirt is one of two that I have left. I wanted to swap it one day but the man didn't want it because it's white and he didn't have any soap. He wanted a dark coloured shirt. I told him he'd find some soap. I was so hungry and I really wanted to exchange this shirt, but he didn't want to know.

We travelled 10 kilometres, and they [the FAA] arrived behind us. We had to set off again. We also ate wild fruits. Some people died. Luckily we found food in the abandoned villages. And that lasted like that until we got to Zambezi. We advanced in a zigzag without knowing where we were going; sometimes people told us which way to go. Then we found that we were not too far from Zambia, so we continued into Zambia in search of some peace. Some people died of bronchitis, of hunger or diarrhoea, of malaria. Two children were bitten by snakes and they also died. Now we are going to wait until our country is better. If there is peace there, we will go back. Even today, I love our country. With your help we can have peace.

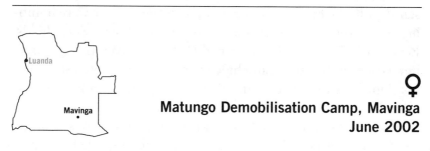

♀
Matungo Demobilisation Camp, Mavinga
June 2002

My mother joined UNITA in 1974. I was born on base number 35 in Huambo Province. I stayed on that base until I was 15 years old. Afterwards I went to the logistical base[27] in 1989 with my big sister. I was married there in 1992 to a man from base number 50 in Benguela Province. In the logistical base we lived well: there was enough food, clothes. I worked in the fields… From 2001 onwards the situation became more difficult. When we were attacked we all ran away together in a group. I was with my husband and my four children. I didn't see the attacks; I just heard the shooting from far away. I left everything behind, our clothes, everything, I couldn't even bring anything to eat. We have not been back to the base to

---

[27] A large base in Cuando Cubango charged with producing food for UNITA's forces in South Eastern Angola.

see what was left there. In the bush we just walked and fled. We didn't have clothes or food. We covered our heads with our hands when it rained. We didn't have time to search for something to eat in the fields. We ate the maize that we found. We didn't have time to hunt or fish. To kill our thirst, when there was no water, we chewed on leaves. The children became anaemic because of the shortage of salt. For two months we would eat one day, and not eat for two days, like that…. We didn't stay in the group, we split up. I ended up on my own with my children because I stopped for a moment. With the children it was difficult to run. My husband managed to escape. I prayed a lot. God helped us. I went as far as Lomba on foot. There, I found some people. They had radios and they told me that no one was fighting any more, that the war was finished. We were really tired. In April we stopped running.

In May, we set off with the FAA on foot from Lomba with a little maize and cassava on our heads, to go to the demobilisation camp of Matungo. There I found my husband again, he had arrived there first. My husband had been given half a cup of rice, and we, the family, received half a cup of rice and a tin and a half of sardines. That was one month ago, and since then we have received nothing more. My husband went to see if he could find something in the fields that we left in the logistical base, but there's nothing left there now, the sweet potatoes and the cassava are finished. We haven't eaten anything in four days. In the demobilisation camp they have started giving out a few clothes as well, but I haven't received anything yet because they haven't yet reached our battalion. There is no one left in the bush. The people who were still there were fetched by trucks last week. Everyone has arrived in the demobilisation camp now; there are already 10 battalions here. Everyone that I knew in the logistical base has already arrived. The ones who haven't arrived are dead. We heard that such a person is dead of sickness or of hunger…We don't know how long we will stay in the demobilisation camp or when the troops will leave here. I would like to go back to Huambo to see my family. My husband will definitely want to go back to his land in Benguela. But with the sickness of my children[28] I can't manage to think about anything. With all of the suffering that they've been through, they've fallen sick

---

[28] One of her children was severely malnourished and receiving nutritional intensive care in an MSF therapeutic feeding centre.

again…I am really so tired of this. I hope that the war is finished (laughs). I hope that my children can live well because they've already suffered too much, too long.

♀
Caala
May 2002

This woman had been brought from Galangue Demobilisation Camp in Huila so that her child could attend an MSF therapeutic feeding centre in Caala.

In Galangue [demobilisation camp] there are many diseases: tuberculosis, anaemia, measles. When I arrived, after the cease-fire in April, there were already a lot of people in Galangue. The people were arriving from all of the UNITA bases in the surrounding area, they were already sick, with their feet swollen up. There were many sick people and many deaths. Before, on the base, it wasn't like this but now that we're all together there are deaths every day – 10 per day or sometimes 20. Not a day goes past without us hearing women weeping for a child that they've just lost. Every day children die. There is nothing to eat. Once we received rice from the government, with one spoon of salt and one spoon of oil, and that was all. Because of that we were eating sweet potatoes that we found in the old abandoned fields in the surrounding area, but they're not good, they're just roots, they weren't planted or cultivated.

I come from a UNITA base close to Samboto. I was born in Caluquembe, in the province of Huila. My mother was a nurse and my father was a deacon in the church. I am 20 years old. I stayed in Caluquembe until I was 15 years old, in 1997. Life there was good, everything went well. Yes, there was war, but we had good land so we didn't suffer much at that time. I got married when I was 15 in Caluquembe and my husband, who was 17 years old, was sent to the UNITA base in Samboto, he was a soldier. In the beginning everything went well on the base, but later on there was a massive government offensive and we lost everything: clothes, blankets, everything. I saw Savimbi a few times. Sometimes he was young, sometimes he was an adult and sometimes he was an old man. He changed his appearance like magic.

The last MPLA attack came after Savimbi's death. There was a big attack by their soldiers and many people died, mostly [UNITA] soldiers but also civilians, because there were civilians who were working the land there to feed us. I managed to escape with my husband, my father and my son. We'd all been living together on the base with my parents. My mother was a nurse there and my father was farming. I also have three brothers, one older and two younger. They're all in Galangue now. I only have one child, who is one year old.[29] I had another one but he died. This one was born on the base. When we ran away from the base there were already many people who were sick. There were no medicines so the people started to get sick and died. We were only eating cassava. We didn't even have time to make flour with the cassava because the [FAA] soldiers from Bunjei were following us non-stop. So we were just eating the cassava like that, without preparing it.

Afterwards we found out that Savimbi and [UNITA deputy President] Dembo had died. So since they were dead we could already talk with the others [from the MPLA side]. We came out of the bush and headed for Galangue which is an area where all the UNITA soldiers are assembling. We are waiting for the government to give us food and seeds. Until now only the soldiers have received some food, but the civilians haven't received anything. Some soldiers are trying to get back in touch with their families, their relatives, to get some help. In Galangue there's a central UNITA command which gives orders to all the people. There is also a boss from the MPLA. They both run things, one from UNITA and one from the MPLA. Afterwards I want to go back to Caluquembe to do something. My husband was wounded in the leg during the war, by a bullet so he can't walk very well. You can tell as soon as you see him.

---

[29] Her baby was severely malnourished and receiving care in an MSF therapeutic feeding centre.

⚲
Saurimo
June 2002

We arrived in the transit camp[30] on April 27 [2002]. Life in the camp is not easy. We lack food, cooking oil. We received some rice and some cassava flour when I arrived, but afterwards, nothing more. To diversify what we eat we swap cassava flour for vegetables. It's one of our neighbours here who prepares our meals: I give her the food and she cooks it for me and my daughter. Before arriving here we were in Lubalo. We walked for 15 days to arrive here, and we had nothing [to eat] on the way. We got a little bit of cassava flour from the local people because sometimes they took pity on the children. We went to the demobilisation camp, but since my wife was ill we were brought here because she didn't have the strength to work or perform domestic tasks.[31]

No one was forced to join UNITA. UNITA did not oppress people; everyone was free to do what he wanted. In the bush there were temporary places where we stayed for a month, maybe more. It depended. In 2000, we stayed in one place for a year, in 2001 for half a year. Wherever we arrived we built huts with the materials we found locally. When the situation permitted, when things were calm, we could grow potatoes. Otherwise we were short of food, of clothes, of medicines. It was a calamity. We were cut off from the urban world, from the humanitarian agencies. When the enemy arrived we had to leave. We were attacked, some people were captured. I found people here in the camp who were captured by the FAA years ago. In UNITA I was a radio operator. They trained me. Now, I want to adapt to the present situation, I'd like to work in telecommunications because I know a bit about computing as well. I am confident that the war is over. Neither UNITA nor the FAA is

---

[30] A camp where the sick and malnourished from the nearby demobilisation camps were brought to receive medical treatment.

[31] This man's wife died of malaria three days after reaching the transit camp. His three-year-old child had died of starvation earlier in 2002. He was left only with his two-year-old child.

in a state to make more war. Everything has come out of the understanding between the two militaries. It's them who decided to make peace. I don't want more war. I want to be a normal citizen. Those who say that UNITA is still hiding men in the bush are wrong. The bush is empty now... I belong to the command of General Sousa e Mosengo. I have been authorised to contact my family. I have relatives in Luanda. I want to contact them to leave them my daughter because the living conditions there are better. I want to ask [the Social Affairs Ministry] MINARS to help me do that. I will try to find work in Saurimo. But if my General orders me to go to the demobilisation camp then I will go.

**Saurimo
June 2002**

On April 23, 2002, I was brought with my family and other people by helicopter from the bush to Saurimo, to the military hospital because I had a muscular disease. I don't know who brought us, if it was soldiers from the FAA or UNITA. I just know that they were pilots. After my operation at the hospital we went to the transit camp, and from there they sent me here[32] with my child. I am from Huambo. In the party...you know, you had to belong to that...I left Huambo in 1992 with the hope of our party, but with a bit of suffering even so. From there I took a plane to the border with Zaire where our commando units were. From there we went to Malange and then on to the Cuango area. That's where we fought until the cease-fire. Life in the bush was easy in the beginning because near the borders people had salt, soap, clothes, a bit of everything. But when the borders were closed[33] life became more difficult for everyone, the conditions were very basic. They were the conditions of war, you know. The men went to fight, the women cultivated maize,

---

[32] To an MSF therapeutic feeding centre for the severely malnourished where his child was being treated.
[33] Following the imposition of UN sanctions on UNITA from 1997 onwards.

sweet potatoes and beans. The men went off to war and when they came back the house was built and the food was ready. We moved a lot. Many people died as well. My children were sick during the war but fortunately none of them died. But after the terrible death of Savimbi – no one expected that, it was a huge surprise – then life got even more complicated. In the base where we were, in Xassengue, we were the Dragon Commandos. We had never been attacked. There were a few engagements sometimes with the FAA, but we responded to them. There were other areas which were attacked a lot more than us. The enemy arrived in our base only after UNITA had left.

Now the time of killing is over. They have laid down their weapons and so have we. Our leaders have discussed and agreed that the suffering is too much, that enough is enough. We are all the same, we are all brothers, we are all Angolans. The people in the bush will all leave the bush and come here. There's not many people left there anyway, either from UNITA or not. People's morale is good: they're thinking about the future, they want to work and forget the past. When my child is better we will go back to the transit camp and from there to the demobilisation camp at Peso. I've heard that there is a shortage of food there, but since those are our orders, the law, we have to go there until the situation improves. After Peso I will return to my family in Huambo. There I am going to buy a house because with demobilisation the troops will be given work and medicines. The government says it is going to help us, but I'm not too sure about that.

♀
Saurimo
June 2002

This woman was interviewed in the MSF feeding centre in Saurimo where one of her children was being cared for.

Before I arrived here I was in the transit camp. My husband

came out of the bush first, with three of my children, and I don't know where he is now, if he's in Luanda or Huambo. I don't know how my three other children are now...I haven't had any news of them. They stayed with my first husband. We separated because he mistreated me. I wonder if they're still alive. I joined UNITA in 1976, out of political conviction. I was 16 then. I was young when the [nationalist] movements emerged. And since we were young, we didn't know politics very well, it was the illusion of youth. Everyone joined a movement – some went to UNITA, others joined the government. The people of Bié mostly joined UNITA. My two sisters were captured [by UNITA] along with some other people when they went out for a walk, they fell into an ambush. And I followed them by joining the movement...I joined up to do a nursing course, but whoever went into the bases, never left again. I met up with my sisters again 10 years ago, but then we were separated again. Maybe they are refugees in Zambia now. When the war started we retreated deep into the bush until 1992. And then, from 1992 onwards, we started withdrawing again, especially since 1999...There, life started to become more difficult. We were being attacked night and day. We were constantly on the run, in the rain, hungry. We ate the cassava which we found in abandoned fields. Some people died, others were captured and taken away...The women have good morale today because the peace has been signed and they have the hope that they will find their families again. I don't necessarily want to return to Bié. At least in the beginning I will stay wherever I can find some work. Later perhaps I'll think of going back to Bié. It's just that I left my area a very long time ago; I know nothing about my family. Where will I be able to stay? As for my other children, I don't know how I will find them again.

I joined UNITA in 1974. At that time there were three parties and every Angolan had to choose one and receive a membership card. When the leaders started not getting on, the people started to suffer. If you were from UNITA, you were in the territory of the others, and vice versa…with the membership cards we couldn't hide which party we belonged to. There were those who stayed in the towns and us others who went into the bush with Savimbi to start the guerrilla war. UNITA's forces are organised…. The FAA arrived in Mavinga in May 2001. Initially the population of Mavinga fled into the bush. Then, when we were also attacked by the FAA, we joined the people of Mavinga to flee along with them. Our village and our fields were burnt. If they hadn't been burnt we would have gone home. In the bush we put up with indescribably miserable conditions. When we were running away everyone ran in a different direction, the children got lost…. I even saw a mother who had to leave behind the child who fell from her back. Really, death would have been preferable.

Why were we born to suffer like that? It was our brothers who made us suffer. When we were captured the FAA told us that they didn't want to kill civilians, that they were going to bring us back to Mavinga…. We had to obey them always, if anyone tried to argue they were decapitated. Those who tried to run away, adults and children, were shot down. I remember some were hiding near the river when they were surprised [by the FAA]. They were killed and thrown in the water. They also raped the women, and they brought those who were widows, or alone without their husbands back to Mavinga, and married them by force.[34] When their husbands came out of the bush and

---

[34] Angolans use this expression to describe situations where women are kidnapped and forced, by soldiers from both armies, to live with them as their wives, even though they are not legally married.

found their wives married to [FAA] soldiers in Mavinga, they couldn't talk to them directly. They had to go through the *soba* who would ask the woman to choose the soldier or the husband. The municipal administration helps also. But often the soldier threatens the woman so that she won't leave, so she rejects her husband out of fear. Some women have managed to escape to go and find their real husbands in the bush. The widows who don't have a husband to come and fetch them just have to keep quiet. Most of the [FAA] soldiers are devils, crazy people with no education. In Mavinga they intimidate us and make trouble. We don't understand what is their job here; we don't see what they do. They drink a lot...and even if they're disarmed, some have knives. Not long ago some soldiers tried to steal a little calf from us during the night because they thought that we were sleeping. They hit the people and threaten them with their knives. They abuse people, women too. They rape them. One night they came and slapped me awake, took me out of my bed, and then had their way with my wife. They even embrace the little girls who are 10, 11, 12 years old. We, the parents, can do nothing; we have no defence against them. If we argue with them, they beat us. If we go and lodge a complaint, and the soldier is found, then he is just told off by his commander. UNITA's troops never raped, they don't rape. Here, FAA troops don't respect anything. Your [MSF's] presence is essential, we prayed for you to arrive. I'd say that they show more respect since you have been here. In the neighbourhoods which are further away they carry on abusing the people.... There are still many people in the bush, but since March no new people have arrived in Mavinga because the FAA don't go to fetch them any more.

The last battles near the logistical base took place in March 2002. The people who are still in bush are afraid to come here because of the bad treatment we receive from the soldiers. That's why we want to return to the interior of the country[35] because maybe there things are calmer. There are many of us here who originate from the provinces of Huambo, Benguela and Huila. All of these people want to go back home, but how? I have my eyes fixed on my land of origin. If there were some means of transport

---

[35] The central provinces of Huambo, Bié, Benguela and Huila.

we wouldn't be here any longer, only the people from Mavinga would still be here. The municipal administration says it will help us. The people who are originally from this province are going back to their villages secretly because they're not well treated here and because they have nothing to eat in Mavinga. The problem is that the food was also burnt in their villages. Others are also running away into the bush to find their families who have stayed there. Me, I would rather die than go back to the bush…. There are many disoriented people who go from the bush to Mavinga, and from Mavinga to the bush. We are dying of hunger here. The people have started preparing their fields for August planting. The land here doesn't belong to anyone, it's a case of first come first served. The administration has given a few cabbage, carrot, spinach and onion seeds. The spinach didn't germinate. The cabbage has started to grow, but people steal it. The Ganguela [local ethnic group] are not farmers. They are hunter-gatherers, nomads by tradition. UNITA tried to teach them agriculture but without much success. Now we think that we have escaped from the war, but it's the war of hunger which is beginning. If we get to July without food there will be death here. If food aid reaches Mavinga a lot of people will come out of the bush. But you [MSF] should

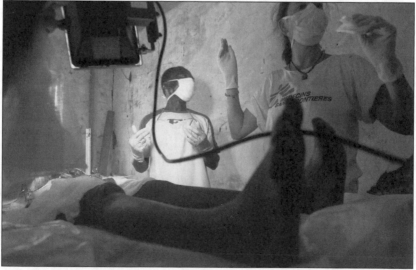

2002 © Alixandra Fenton

An MSF midwife assisting a local surgeon in the makeshift operating theatre in the ruins of Mavinga Government hospital. Mavinga 2002.

take charge of all of that because if you entrust it to the leaders here the aid will never get to the people. If only we had some serious leaders, but they're all corrupt. Savimbi was a charismatic man; he did everything for the good of the people. But his adjutants were corrupt and favoured their own families.

If the Portuguese brothers[36] hadn't left we would be enjoying life today. The Portuguese brothers resolved problems, they discussed things well. But the Angolan brothers who stayed behind don't resolve anything. Misery has increased. Now, if you [MSF] abandon us we will all disappear. Only the strongest will be left... We don't know if the war is over, we have our doubts. But I believe that this time it's really over. We have confidence when we see you. Our hearts are calm because now the white brothers have arrived with medicine and food... We don't want any more war. It's better like it is now. It makes no sense – one leader who pushes the people this way, another who pushes them the other way. Anyone who starts a war ought to be punished because it destroys everything. Everything disappears – men, goods. War is devastating; it respects nothing, not even God. Even the churches were destroyed and the people killed inside them.

Now, in school and in the families we are explaining to the children that it's peace, and that peace brings well-being, that everyone must go to school and receive an education. Some parents send their children to school because they know the value of things, but others are still ready to take up arms. The majority of the children of school age don't go to school here. School started in April, but there are only 1005 students registered, and 27 teachers. The government gave out a few exercise books, but there aren't enough for everyone.... There, in our land of origin, our families are crying for us, and here we are crying for them. How can we make contact with them? Those who stayed at home will welcome us back there, we will all be reconciled. But how can we get there without any means of transport? People here talk with the traders who come to sell things in the market. They ask: "Where did you come from. Do you know so and so? Is he still alive?" When the trader comes back the next time people give him letters to deliver. Every day people from Mavinga

---

[36] The colonial administration.

wait for the military truck to arrive so they can go to Menongue to look for their relatives.

♀
12-year-old orphan
Mavinga
June 2002

I was born in Jamba. So were my brothers. We were there with our family. There, I used to go to school…. We left Jamba to go to Licua. I don't know what happened – we were attacked and we ran away with our aunt. My parents left us a very long time ago, us five children. I don't know where they are. In the bush I was afraid. We didn't have any food; we were eating roots and leaves. It was cold and we didn't have any blankets. I wore the clothes that I'm still wearing now. We ran all the time. We walked on sticks and hurt our feet. There was shooting all the time and they [the FAA] threw the children in the rivers. Afterwards they found us in the bush. I arrived here a long time ago, on foot with the [FAA] soldiers. I arrived after the other orphans, along with my little brothers. When I got here I was treated in the hospital. The soldiers gave us this tent because the rains are going to arrive and we're going to get wet. Everyone in our tent is here with brothers and sisters. It's our "uncle"[37] who looks after us. The soldiers gave us a bit to eat – some rice, some wheat, some beans, some tins of meat and fish. But today we have been given nothing because there's nothing left. We don't know when we will eat again. We watch the trucks full of soldiers passing and we wait. The "aunties"[38] bring us a little maize flour from the town, that's all. We, the elder children, do the washing, we make food. We cook the maize flour and leaves from the sweet potato plants, with no salt or oil. The little children just eat and play. Later on I don't know what I will do. Nothing.

---

[37] A teacher who was caring for the orphans.
[38] Local ladies helping to provide for the orphans.

♀
9-year-old orphan
Mavinga
June 2002

This child was interviewed in an MSF therapeutic feeding centre where she was being treated.

I came from far away, from Tembo, Capembe, with my mother. We set off to take refuge in Zambia, in a camp. While we were running with lots of people, I got lost. It was my aunt, the sister of my mother, who found me again…. After I got lost I was all on my own, with the rain and the cold. I slept alone. I ate wild fruits from the forest and sand. There was nothing to eat. I walked all the time, my feet hurt. I never saw any soldiers but I heard the bombs far away. I was afraid. It was my aunt who brought me here, but I didn't come to go to hospital (she's obviously confused). What will I do now? The other lady who has taken me in is a trader. She says that she will keep me and take me to Cuito.

Kidnapped by UNITA

♀
Mavinga
June 2002

I left Moxico in 1982. I was captured by UNITA when they attacked our village; they took away a group of 80 girls. In the beginning I was in the bush in Moxico, then, in 1986, I came to Mavinga. I studied in the high school in the base at Licua until I was 15. I couldn't study any longer because there were no more of the white teachers (she can't remember their nationality) who used to come and give courses in vaccination and nutrition, like in 1992 when there was the mini-peace. Life in the bases was just suffering. When we were little we used to be given food by the state [UNITA]. The population suffered, it was only the senior ranking men who received good food, like meat, and ate well. When we were a bit older they put us in the houses of the grown ups, the officers. There, we had to work, washing the clothes, but they didn't give us anything, no clothes, no food. Some of those officers raped the young girls, so they ran away. I stayed three years in the house of an officer. I was well treated because he had a wife from Moxico, so nothing happened to me. Sometimes the soldiers also did things. I remember one young girl who was on her way back from the fields when she found herself face to face with a UNITA soldier. He beat her, grabbed her, stuffed his hat into her mouth, and raped her. People say that that man was killed for that, but they also say that the girl went mad.... In 1987, my parents were also captured. They were sent to the logistical base of Mavinga where they farmed the land. There were lots of people there. A lot of the people who are now in Mavinga in the demobilisation camps here used to be in the logistical base. My husband is from Kwanza Sul, but he had to go to Huambo for work and he's never come back. So, I took my children and went to live with my parents. I lived with them for 10 years. Afterwards the population was divided up and I was sent to Jamba with the children. Since I wasn't working in the fields I had to cope by trading, otherwise we'd have had nothing to eat, nothing to wear, because we were receiving nothing from the state. I used to sell clothes from Namibia until we were attacked and everything I owned was stolen.

The FAA attacked us on December 18, 2000, but they didn't find anybody there because everyone had already withdrawn into the bush or to the refugee camps in Zambia. I ran and hid in the bush, there was a big group of us. We split up so that we wouldn't all go to the same base. One group was sent to the base of Lomba, another to the base at Capembe, and another to the base of Luangundo. We were sent to the base at Rivungo, near the River Kuando and the Zambian border. Then, while I was visiting my parents, there was an attack on the logistical base on May 8, 2001, so all of the people had to run away in the night. I was in the bush with lots of people and my parents. We slept one night here, one night there. We were just running all the time. The pregnant women were also running, but if they couldn't keep it up they handed themselves in [to the FAA]. The women were afraid of being captured because FAA soldiers raped them and brought them back to Mavinga to marry them by force.... In the bush we were looking for something to eat, some maize, in the fields which we found by abandoned villages. But we had to take care not to get caught by the FAA.... Everyone was going back to the villages looking for food. There were no more clothes. We were carrying the children in blankets because we had no more carrying cloths.[39] My child fell ill in the bush; he had malaria and diarrhoea and we had no medicines so the nurse gave him traditional medicines, some roots. He died on April 21 [2002]. A lot of children died, every day three or four died. A lot of children were also lost when we were running away and were never found again. They died there. In our group there was one child who stayed on her own for six days, she very nearly died, but she had the luck to find a little water. A man from our group found her sitting in the bush and brought her back to her mother….she was all thin…. I spoke to my parents to get them to hand themselves over along with my children because I couldn't go to the demobilisation camp. Women can only go there if they have a husband. So my parents and my children were captured and taken to the demobilisation camp of Matungo. But there also, it's just suffering. There is no salt, there is lots of disease. The children die because there are no medicines. I arrived in Mavinga alone, after the peace. When I joined my family in Matungo demobilisation camp I saw that they were suffering too much, so I left my parents and my two children to come and work in Mavinga town. I have been here for one month. Here, the [FAA] soldiers make trouble when they're drunk. They drink a lot. They beat the people. When a soldier doesn't want the woman that he married by force in the bush, he takes her clothes and everything, and leaves her with nothing, with no home, in the street. I have an aunt who was beaten. The soldier took everything from her and left her with nothing. They also marry by force girls as young as 12. They get married, but then afterwards the soldiers don't do anything. It's the woman who has to go and find food, and do everything else. Now, as it's peacetime, I'd say that the soldiers talk a bit more, and behave like that a bit less.

---

[39] Angolan women use large rectangles of material, called *panos*, both as wrap-around skirts, and to tie their small children on their backs.

From 1978 until 1981 I lived in Mavinga. At that time the town hadn't yet been destroyed by the UNITA occupation, it was under the control of the MPLA. On March 13, 1981, UNITA came and destroyed the town. The whole population that was here was taken into the bush for 20 years. I went into the bush in 1981 and only came back out again in 2001. I was captured with my mother. Some people managed to run away to Menongue, to Cuito, or to Zambia. The people who were captured were split up. The first base where we lived was called 13th March Canga. It was a satellite base of Licua, because Licua was a larger base, a bit like Jamba which was the provisional capital of UNITA. There, life was difficult – there was no food in the beginning when we first occupied the area. People ate wild fruits from the forest and game meat. Sometimes the leadership of UNITA helped the population with some food rations, but it was not enough because life as a guerrilla is a complicated life. In the beginning, we ate in community kitchens because there was not much food, and there were a lot of people to be fed. After two years some seeds and agricultural implements appeared, and people were spread out to cultivate the land, outside the satellite bases, but still under the control of the bases. After that the kitchens were turned into schools. In the beginning I didn't do anything. I started studying in 1983, when Jamba started sending schools to the satellite bases. After that I was sent to the Polyvalent College.[40] But as my health was a bit fragile I went home often to my family, so I stopped after the fourth class. When I stopped studying I was appointed to be a teacher for the young children. Because of my health problems I was never given military training.

I married in Canga, but my first daughter was born at

---

[40] A sort of high school run by UNITA.

Luangundo, and the second at Lomba because after my mother was killed by witchcraft in Canga I didn't want to stay there any longer. In December 1999, I went to Lomba, to live in a village where my second father[41] was *soba*. Today he is still here with me in Mavinga. My biological father is in Cuito Cuanavale with his second wife and my elder brothers. I haven't seen him since I was a child. In Lomba in 1999, we used to get goods from merchants in exchange for diamonds. They came from Zambia and Namibia to exchange salt, clothes and chickens for diamonds. A lot of people were searching for diamonds in that region. With my health I couldn't join them. On April 7, 2000, the offensive, which I will call "cleansing", hit Lomba. The leaders of UNITA had informed us that the government troops were on their way, well armed, to attack us, and that we should run into the bush. We didn't know what those troops could do to us – would they let us live, or would they kill us on the pretext that we had cooperated with UNITA? So we obeyed the order to abandon the bases, our fields, our homes. When the FAA soldiers arrived there was not a soul left in the town of Lomba. In the bush we spent months without adequate food. We went to search for water at night. When we were hungry, and the way was clear, four or five men would go to the abandoned fields to look for maize or cassava. Some tried to fish a bit as well. Everything was dangerous, we were risking our lives every minute. A lot of people were captured when they were going to look for food or water. A lot died as well: some were shot because they refused to turn themselves in, others died of disease, of malaria, or swollen legs, or of hunger and thirst because they couldn't find the river. When things were calm those people were buried, otherwise they just rotted away where they were. Those who couldn't bear it any more turned themselves in so that they could come to Mavinga and rest. FAA troops chased us through the bush until they captured us. On November 30, 2001, they found my uncle, his wife, my wife and my children on the right bank of the River Lomba. Afterwards I stayed with another man, but then I thought, why stay here without my family? So I came on my own to Mavinga, I walked for two hours. It was only when I got to Mavinga that I understood what the FAA wanted to do:

---

[41] Paternal Uncle.

they were gathering together all of the people to put them under the control of the government, to tell them that they had already spent too long in the bush and that it was time to come back together to build our Angola. I had been wishing for a long time that I could return to Mavinga to find my family, my brothers and cousins, who had remained in the government areas. Everybody had had enough of not being free, of living under the trees for so many years. So when the people understood that the government troops were preparing to gather together all of the people so that they could live under government control, a lot of people rejoiced. Even UNITA soldiers laid down their arms and came here of their own accord because they were tired. In the beginning I believed in UNITA's doctrine. But as time went by I realised that things were going on and on, that they never ended, and so I realised that it wasn't working. No one was born to suffer all year, people are born to be free. Since the election of 1992 I began to have my doubts, and to feel the urge to see my family again. That year, everybody in Cuando Cubango was free and happy that the war was over, that we could be free, lead a normal life, and go home. Afterwards, we saw that things began to change. Some people were happy to carry on living according to UNITA's doctrine, but others, the majority, were tired. We knew that we were from UNITA because UNITA controlled us, because they had found us here and brought us into their party, but inside ourselves we felt free, independent, we felt that we were from Cuando Cubango.... I was happy to return to Mavinga. The problem is the behaviour of the FAA. Before, the soldiers took people's saucepans, their animals; they insulted the women and the old people. Now they have calmed down a bit. It is you [MSF] who have liberated us. When they went to round up the people in the bush they raped the girls who they found on their own and brought them here to marry them by force. There are very few soldiers who don't have a woman. Many of the women became pregnant, and lots of the women were subsequently abandoned when the soldiers had satisfied their needs.... The commander is trying to stamp out all of that, so things are getting a bit better. But some individuals don't take any notice and carry on like that.... When I arrived in Mavinga the government gave me a little food, some cassava flour. They also gave out some clothes and blankets, a bit of oil and some soap, but it wasn't enough for everyone. Since December, when I arrived, until the end of May my family survived on the cassava that we found in the Lomba area. But now there's none left there. So what are we going to eat? Since the seeds and tools have not arrived, we cannot prepare the fields for August. Some people go to pick wild fruits, any kind of food that they can find in the bush. The government is everything; everyone is waiting for the government to give more support to us, the people of Mavinga. That's a collective complaint. We feel that the WFP[42] should come here soon; they have to come and help the people. The people's biggest worry is hunger because we cannot stand more hunger. Apart from that, their other wish is to be able to live like before, like in 1978, 1979. The civil servants could stay here, and the ordinary people could return to their fields and resume their responsibilities. We know that everything will take time, but we have hope, the hope that everything will turn out okay.

♂

Nangweshi Refugee Camp, Zambia
February 2001

I grew up in Benguela, which is a beautiful city by the sea, but I haven't seen the sea for many years. Life was normal until I was 16. Then, one day, on my way home from school, I was picked up by a FAPLA press gang. They forced me onto a truck, took me and lots of other boys to the airport, and flew us in a big cargo plane to Luanda. I didn't even have the chance to go home first. My parents didn't know what had happened to me. They put me through military training near Luanda, and then sent me to the front. I was in the infantry. It was two years before I managed to contact my family to tell them I was alive. In 1986, I was based in Cubal in

---

[42] The United Nations World Food Programme.

Benguela Province. There was a lot of fighting in that area. One day, early in the morning, UNITA attacked the town. Our forces retreated but I got caught in a UNITA ambush. They took me prisoner. After the attack UNITA forces withdrew back into the bush, a few days march away. They kept me tied up. Then they decided to send me to their headquarters in Jamba. We walked for two months to get there, on small tracks in the bush that only UNITA knew. There were other prisoners with us, and anyone who resisted or complained was killed. We walked for about eight hours a day, sleeping under the trees. We had mostly only honey and wild fruits to eat.

When we got near Jamba they sent me to a camp called *Nova Aurora* (New Dawn). They called it a "re-education camp" for political prisoners. It was hell. For the first two months they put me in a prison under the ground. They dug a big pit, covered it over with branches and earth so that it was completely dark inside, and then built a hut over the top of it. There were many people in there, sitting squashed together in the dark. We had to relieve ourselves in that pit. People went mad, some people went blind, some died. We had to bury the ones who died in the floor of the pit. After two months they took me out of the pit. The light hurt,

2000 © Jet Belgraver

Over 3000 Angolan refugees fled across the border to Sillilimwe refugee camp set up by MSF in Kalabo, Zambia. Kalabo 2000.

I could hardly see. Then they put me to work. Every day we started work at dawn, clearing fields and planting. Each prisoner had
to clear a certain area every day. If you didn't manage it, you were
beaten. We worked the whole day without a break and without
eating. In the late afternoon they gave us something to eat. Then
we had to go and prepare food and do housework for UNITA soldiers who ran the camp. After that they made us listen to political
lectures for two, three hours – about how UNITA would win the
war and transform Angola, and how Savimbi would be President.
If you fell asleep they would beat you. After that they made us
dance and sing songs about UNITA until late into the night. You
had to look like you were enjoying yourself or they punished you.
Then they put us back in the pit until the next day. I did that every
day for two years. After two years they said I was re-educated.
They sent me to live in Jamba, to work as a teacher. I was stuck
there until December 1999. No one could leave that place, not
even UNITA people. UNITA police killed people whom they
caught running away. There was a lot of fear.

In 1992, there was peace and Angola had elections. We were so
happy; we thought we would be able to go home. The
[International Committee of the] Red Cross came to Jamba to
take letters to our families.[43] They said they would come back to
take the political prisoners home but just before they came back
UNITA hid almost all of us in camps in the bush. They just handed a few over to the Red Cross and said the rest of us preferred to
stay with them. It was a lie, but there was nothing we could do....
That was a bad time. We didn't have another chance to escape
until 1999 when the FAA reached Jamba for the first time. They
came with MIGs and helicopters and bombed us. Everyone ran
away. We couldn't hand ourselves over to them, they came shooting and they would have killed us. There were more FAA soldiers
blocking the way across the border. These people who are here in
this camp are the ones who managed to get across the border.
Most of the people from Jamba got stuck in Angola in the bush. I
walked for two weeks to get to the border. We had to cross a big
river and many people drowned. Then we reached Zambia. Here
in this camp there are many of the people who ran Jamba – the

---

[43] The ICRC runs a family tracing and reunification programme for those who have lost
touch with their relatives. As part of this service they deliver letters to loved ones.

head of the police, the head of the prisons. And then there are people like me. We are meant to be refugees, to be protected, but we are living here with the people who captured us and tortured us. Now they run this camp. I am sick of this life in the bush. I just want to go home to Benguela, but how? How can I get there? I'm sure my family must think that I'm dead.

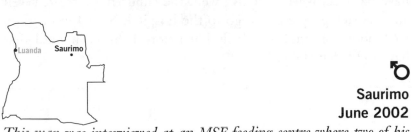

Saurimo
June 2002

This man was interviewed at an MSF feeding centre where two of his four children were receiving treatment.

It took me three days to walk to Peso [demobilisation camp] from the place in Lunda Norte Province where I was. As my child was sick, I came here to the hospital at the beginning of June. I entered UNITA in 1980. I was captured along with some other people from my village, including some of my younger brothers and some uncles. We were divided up according to our ages. As I was 14 at the time, I was sent to Jamba to study a bit. But I didn't stay there long. I only spent two years in school, and then when I was 17 I was sent to the training camp in Lunda Norte. I left there in 1987 to go out into the provinces.... Until 1992, life was better. There were free areas conquered by UNITA. In 1992, things started going backwards.... After the sanctions were imposed on UNITA things started to change and the crisis began. We really became guerrillas. Our army didn't receive any more support from the party. It depended completely on itself and on the abilities of the commander in the region.... Food depended on the local people. We ate fish, meat, and the cassava harvest abandoned by the people. We fled from the government attacks and no one was captured. I had a brother who was killed in 2001 in the war. We wanted to put up a fight but there was no time. We mistrusted the government. The first message that we received in 2001 came on December 17, 2001. Doctor Savimbi had made a speech to the nation in favour of peace. And then, on February 22, we heard about his death. From then on the two chiefs of staff started to meet to begin this phase [of peace]. The militant people [UNITA] were complaining about this war, and wondering when it was going to end. So when we heard about the cease-fire there was much joy…. We get on fine with the others [the FAA], they have received us well, we live well, the children are treated well and the sick people get to go to the hospital. Now I want to go back home and find my family but before I can go home I first have to be demobilised.

⚦

**Saurimo
June 2002**

In 1984, when I was on my way to visit my parents-in-law with my wife and children, we were captured by UNITA. I am a metal-worker, so in UNITA I was making spades for diamond mining, and cutlery. That was my job, working at the forge. From 1999 to 2000, we were based in Alto Chicapa. Everyone had their job. My wife worked in the fields and fished, other people were miners. If someone had his own stone [diamond] he could trade it, but the diamonds which belonged to the State [UNITA] could not be touched. The diamonds were sent straight to President Savimbi, and we received half of the money [from their sale]. With that we used to buy sugar, salt, fish, rice, bread, ammunition, shoes, from the Congolese along the borders but recently everything has been closed off [because of the UN sanctions on UNITA]. But the Congolese had their own routes they used to come in secretly. Everything got more difficult from 2001 onwards when the [FAA] offensive started. The soldiers ran out of ammunition, we had to run away and order the women to hide. Lately we didn't even have a chance to grow anything…we were eating leaves and cassava flour which we got by exchanging all of our clothes and metal – which could be melted down to make cooking pots. Those who were strong or scared enough sought refuge in Congo, in a village for Angolan refugees. But I am an Angolan, so whether they kill me or not, it's better for me to die here, in Angola. At Lachimba, beyond the River Luxico, there's a village. We marched for one day, the sick people for a day and a half, to get there. That's where we were captured by the FAA. Afterwards they brought us to Capaia by car. From Capaia I was taken to Lucapa, and from there to Saurimo because I was sick. I came with all of my family so they could be checked out because I have tuberculosis.... Since I've already worked a lot in Moxico, and studied as far as the seventh class, I know how to fix watches, how to build houses, how to work with metal, and I'm a really good mechanic. If I get better, we will see what the government will do to put us in jobs which we know how to do. If they tell me to go back to my home area, I will go. If they tell me to stay here, I will stay. We live like neighbours with the people of Saurimo.... Wherever they tell me to go.... I am waiting for orders. Now the war is over. War is something that destroys. Before we accepted nothing from the enemy, but now the only thing we want is peace. It was a fight between brothers. Our superiors have analysed the situation well, and they have explained to us that we must let all of that go now. We're here, we're brothers and we've been well received. They give us the same food as they eat.

♀
Caala
May 2002

This woman was interviewed in an MSF therapeutic feeding centre where two of her children were receiving treatment.

We suffered a lot in the forest, with no salt, no food, no clothes. I am from Cafunfu [in Lunda Norte province]. I have four children and my husband died in March 2001 in Sector 1. In 1977, my husband was the local delegate for internal commerce.[44] Afterwards, there was a UNITA attack and they kidnapped us. I was 14 at the time, and I was pregnant. They took us to Luena and put us in prison. I was always being watched by the soldiers. After six months they gave me a bit more freedom. Later on we went to Munege, near to Luena. From then, that was in 1978, we stayed in the forest for 12 years just eating wild fruits.

In 1990, we wanted to go to Cafunfu but there wasn't real peace, and on the way we were detained once again by other soldiers from UNITA who prevented us from continuing with our journey. We had to stay with them. They took us to a base. There we planted crops, but we couldn't harvest them because there were attacks all of the time and we were always on the move, always having to change place. By 1990 I had three children, but one got sick and died. My husband died in March 2001, following an attack by the FAA – he was shot in the leg. I managed to carry him to the base but, as he'd lost a lot of blood and there was no doctor and no medicines, he died the next day. I had to carry on following the group of UNITA people. We ate dried bananas; we made flour out of them. In December 2001, the head of the FAA in Chipindo sent soldiers into the forest and I was captured by them. They brought me to Chipindo. There, they gave four kilograms of flour to the people who did not belong to UNITA. I stayed for a month in Chipindo and, afterwards, I went to Bunjei, accompanied by the FAA soldiers because there were UNITA zones and we weren't allowed to go on our own. I went in January 2002 because the children were sick. We went to the health post but we were far too late – they already had oedema. So an MSF car came and picked us up in Bunjei and brought us here, at the end of March. I came with my two sick children, the other one in is Cantão [IDP camp] staying in the house of a friend who came to fetch him. Now one of my two children is already better, he has been discharged. The other one is still being treated. I am well treated here. Later on, since I have no family in Bunjei, I would like to go back to Cafunfu, but I have no money for the journey. I think I will go to Ngove because I know somebody who lives there.

---

[44] A position in the MPLA socialist government.

♀
Caala
May 2002

I was born in Caala. I studied until the seventh class, when I was 15. I have three brothers and four sisters. Life in Caala was nice. In 1994, when I was on my way back from Ngove where I'd gone with my mother to fetch maize from my grandmother's field, we were caught by some soldiers from UNITA. My mother was beaten and they stole all of her clothes. I was kidnapped by the soldiers with 15 other girls who were travelling with us. We were taken, on foot, to a UNITA base close to Bimbe. We stayed there from 1994 to 1996 with very little to eat. All of the girls were forced to marry. I married a soldier who worked in logistics, and came from Huambo. I stayed with him all this time. I was not raped by other men, but other girls who were with me were abandoned by their husbands, and for them things were much harder. In Bimbe we

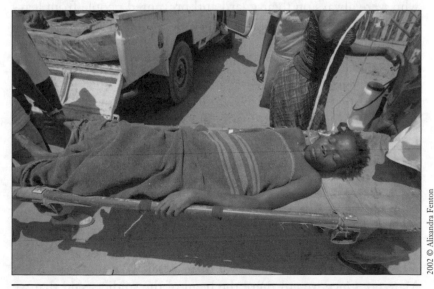

2002 © Alixandra Fenton

After losing her 2 sons to malnutrition, a woman in a nearby village is brought into Mavinga hospital by pickup truck after an attempted suicide. Mavinga 2002.

did all of the work for the soldiers – we made the food, did the washing, etc. But we weren't allowed to eat the food that we prepared, we were only allowed to eat cassava leaves. In 1997, I went with my husband to Andulo where we stayed until 1999. Life there was harder than in Bimbe, the attacks never seemed to stop. In 1999 we had to run away from Andulo with UNITA. We went to Moxico Province. From one minute to the next we had no more food, no more salt. In the beginning we exchanged the clothes that we'd taken with us for salt, after that, nothing. We would travel without stopping for a week, then we'd stop to rest for one day, before setting off again with the FAA on our tail. We walked for over two months with the FAA behind us, bombing us, until we reached eastern Moxico, near Zambia. We were with a huge group of UNITA people. There were five commanders, each with 2 – 3,000 men under their command, with civilians amongst them who could not run away. Those who turned back were killed by the soldiers.

When we got close to Zambia, near Lumbala N'guimbo, we managed to escape persecution by the FAA and stayed for two years in a rearguard UNITA base, in the middle of the forest. There was nobody there. We were surrounded by UNITA soldiers who were always on their guard and prevented people from leaving. There were over a thousand people in that place – prisoners. To eat there was honey and mushrooms in the forest, that was all, and that was what saved us. We exchanged the honey for flour, and my husband went to work in the fields of the people of that region so that we could have flour. I looked after the children. From 2001 onwards the guards became less vigilant and a few people managed to escape in the direction of Menongue, while others handed themselves over to the MPLA. In the end we didn't even have clothes to cover ourselves with.

In 2001, there were frequent attacks by the FAA. The people who didn't run away were taken by them. I was captured with my children on December 17, 2001. My husband had gone into the forest to look for honey when the FAA arrived and, since then, I've never heard from him again. After the attack we went to the River Matemo. Once we got there the head of the soldiers said that we should wait for my husband. He sent the *soba* to fetch him and to tell him that nothing bad would happen to him, but the *soba* didn't manage to convince him because, since he was from UNITA, he was afraid that they would murder him.

They took us with them, along with the children, they helped us to walk. I hadn't had any clothes for months, and they gave me clothes and food. We went to Mupeco, we walked for four days. From there a truck took us to Menongue, where we arrived on December 26, 2001. There we were taken to a refugee [IDP] camp. They gave us blankets, cooking implements, clothes, food, and they gave me a shack for me and my children. After that I asked them for permission to go to the city to try to get in contact with my parents. My children were sick, they had diarrhoea and vomiting. In Menongue I stayed under a tree. A lady showed me a neighbourhood where people from Huambo lived and there I met some people who I knew from before. I stayed there for two weeks – my children were treated in the hospital – and I met a girl who I knew from Caala, we had studied together. She sent a message to my parents, and my mother came to fetch me, via Luanda, in February, in the MSF plane. The children were still sick, especially the little one who is two years old and only weighed five kilograms. Since 1999 I have suffered a lot, from hunger and shortages of everything.

♀
Saurimo
June 2002

This woman was interviewed in an MSF therapeutic feeding centre where one of her two children was being treated.

UNITA used to come and work in my village and in others.... They used to talk with the men; I don't know what they used to say.... Sometimes they took away the women and brought them back at night. I entered UNITA in 1992. My husband had gone to Luanda. They captured me by force, along with some other people, but later on they separated us. I don't know how many soldiers came. I don't know what they did to my village. Afterwards they kept me and we started to be oppressed... (She did not want to go into details) We went to Huambo first. In the beginning life was not suffering – we ate food with oil, rice, we hunted and fished and we had clothes and soap...we lived well. In 1994, I married a man from Bié. Afterwards we went up to the Congolese border, from 1995 to 1998. That's where two of my children died from malaria...there was no medicine. Then, in 1999 the crisis started. When the [FAA] troops attacked we just gathered our things and ran, gathered and ran.... We women ran fast as well...we were afraid because we didn't know what they would do to us...the men...we didn't know what they did to the women they captured, if they beat them or punished them.... We never found those women again, they could be dead today.... I don't know.... I arrived in Peso [demobilisation camp] in May in an FAA truck and later on I was brought here with my child. They found us close to a village, we were walking there. When my child is better I will go back to Peso, and afterwards I don't know what I will do. I don't know if I want to go back to my home area; I don't know if I still have any family there.

♀
Saurimo
June 2002

I have five children who are in Huambo, the five oldest. They are there with my family. I set off with the smaller ones and my husband to trade some food, some beans, in the Malange area. That's where UNITA captured us in 1998. My husband was killed in the bush, on November 9, 2001, while we were running away.... When they called the President [Savimbi] – and he didn't want to go to Luanda to make peace – that's when the big offensive started, which lasted until the people started coming out of the bush. When the big offensive started I got lost and so did my children. They stayed on their own with no food, no fire, nothing, until the FAA came to fetch us out of the bush. Afterwards I was taken to Chicapa and from there I was transferred to the hospital. In the bush life was suffering. We couldn't do anything, we didn't know the area. And even if you tried to escape then UNITA, and even the government troops, would kill you. So we had to run away [from FAA attacks]. We couldn't stay long in the same place because the offensive was never far away. If the offensive caught you…shooting, shooting, shooting, in that shooting if you didn't run you died. Or you died whilst running away, or you died in the base. Afterwards we went on, with the hunger, we didn't have the time to cook. The rain was falling on us; there were no houses…always suffering. No clothes, no blankets, nothing. Sometimes, when things calmed down, we had some time to grow some maize, some beans, some potatoes, some cabbages. We used to have goats, chickens and pigs but when we ran we didn't have the time to take anything with us. The FAA took everything, the food, the clothes, and when we went back to the base there was nothing left there. During the times when we were running away we would spend two or four days without eating. We couldn't light a fire because then the enemy would see us. We stayed under the rain, without moving, under a tree. That's how the diseases started, the anaemia…. Maybe we would find some wild fruit, some water…. That's why I got so I no longer had the strength to walk, I got lost and I lost my children. My toenails fell out, my feet were full of wounds; I couldn't walk any more. Day and night I was crying, until the FAA found me and took me to Chicapa. UNITA left the slow ones behind, lots were left to die. Sometimes UNITA even killed them so that they wouldn't betray them, so that they wouldn't say where the group was headed so that the FAA could catch them. The FAA treated me very well. They gave us food and when I had recovered a bit I went to talk to the commander to tell him that I wanted to find my children. When I got here I found my smallest daughter. She came here all on her own. And another one is in the camp of Ivatengo. Now I need to recover my strength, especially since my home in Huambo is far from here. My stomach hurts, so does my chest, so does my head. But once I am better, and my children too, I will go back there. My family is there, and my other children (laughs).

♀

10-year-old girl
Saurimo
June 2000

The daughter whom the mother has just found following their separation.

Life in the bush was suffering. When I arrived here I was sick, I was anaemic and all swollen up. I walked a lot. It was daytime when we were attacked – afterwards we just had to run, leaving all our things behind. My mother was not there when we were attacked. I was with my brother. Then, my brother went to look for some food. Then they [the FAA] said that their base was in Saurimo. On the way – I came on my own – without eating, I wasn't given anything. I didn't have a cooking pot or a plate. (Her mother adds, "You didn't have a mother either.") I stayed behind at Mana Quimbungo. I found myself on my own at night with a fever. The FAA soldiers brought me in a car. When I got here I was given some food. A lady from the camp took me to the hospital. When I saw my mother I was happy, I cried. Now I am eating well…. I'm not thinking about it any more (laughs). In Huambo I want to go to school. I want to be a doctor (laughs). (Her mother adds "When we get back to Huambo we will start farming, to earn some money so we can buy school books.")

ⵔ ♀
Brother and sister, aged 6 and 7
Malange
December 2000

In their last attack, in March 1999, we were taken by UNITA. They also took our mother, another woman, and our two-year-old brother. We were taken past Cangandala to a place where we lived with UNITA. After some time our mother became sick and died. Right after that UNITA took our little brother down to the river and drowned him because he was always crying for our mother. We lived with the other women until one night when we escaped with a group of other people. During the time we lived with UNITA we were afraid. We were afraid of being killed as we had seen it happen to many other people.

ⵔ
15-year-old boy
Matala
February 2001

I came here last week with my sister. We came from Jamba.[45] We are from Kuvango. It was just my mother and sister and me. My father died of a sickness. One night UNITA came and attacked the town. They took many things from the people and I was taken by UNITA to carry the things they had taken from the people to their base in Chinoca.

I stayed there for two months before I escaped. Nothing happened when I was there. They threatened us that if we tried to escape they would kill us. I met a friend there, so we just spent the days walking around together. I was not afraid. After two months I

---

[45] The small town in Huila Province, not UNITA's former headquarters.

escaped. My friend stayed there because he was born there. His father was a UNITA soldier. I escaped by myself. I spent four days and nights in the bush alone, before I reached Kuvango. I found my sister and my mother and we left and went to Jamba. We stayed there and my mother died of a sickness. My sister and I left there to go to Matala and the government sent us here. We have no family here but there is a school and I will do sixth grade this year.

2002 © Ton Koene

A child admitted to MSF feeding centre is waiting in the kitchen for food. Malange 2002.

"Here and there, it's all the same. Here there is starvation, and there, terror. If you ran into UNITA they'd accuse you of supporting the government and kill you. And if you ran into the FAA they'd accuse you of belonging to UNITA and kill you."

– Male. Chilembo. May 2002.

Part III
Trapped in the Middle

With each phase of Angola's war, and with each failed peace process, an increasing number of Angolans have found themselves in the unenviable position of being trapped between the two belligerents, attacked by both and protected by neither.

As countless of these stories confirm, throughout the war both the government and UNITA viewed anyone who had lived with the "enemy" with suspicion and animosity. They ignored the fact that most Angolans had no choice which party they lived with and that, once living in an area dominated by one belligerent or the other, they had no choice but to support that party. If a person lived with the enemy then they were the enemy. So long as civilians lived with one party and had no contact with the enemy they were relatively safe. However, if they had the misfortune to live in an area which was controlled first by one belligerent and then by the other, they found themselves viewed as traitors and targets by both. The longer the war went on, the more people fell into this category.

During wartime, villages changed hands with the ebb and flow of the fighting. During the peace processes UNITA handed over many areas under their control to government administration. At the approach of government troops during wartime, or government administrators in peacetime, UNITA tried to force all civilians to withdraw with them into the bush. Those who remained behind were subsequently regarded as traitors. UNITA attacked them, stole their belongings and burnt their houses. For their part, advancing into formerly UNITA-controlled areas, the FAA regarded any civilians they found as UNITA supporters. They too tried to force them to leave, to go and live in the cities. If they resisted, the FAA attacked them, stripped them of their possessions, and burnt their houses and crops. In many cases the FAA would forcibly gather civilians together in areas under their control, thereby turning them into targets in the eyes of UNITA. Then, as soon as UNITA attacked, the FAA would retreat, abandoning the civilians to be punished by UNITA for having obeyed the FAA. Anybody who attempted to remain in these beleaguered, transitional villages was viewed as fair game by both armies. Their villages were regularly attacked and pillaged by both sides. If either army caught them tending to their fields, they were accused of growing food to support the "enemy." Neither party provided them with any services – they had no access to schools, health care, or any kind of administrative support. And aid agencies like MSF could not help them because it was too dangerous for us to work in these "grey zones." By the end of the war most of Angola had become a grey zone.

Those who attempted to survive under these dismal conditions describe a sub-human existence. Many speak of being forced to live like "rats" or "monkeys." Most resorted to abandoning their homes in the village and going to live in the forests that ringed their fields. They lived in small shelters, or even in holes, in the bush. During the day they hid from both armies. At night they would sneak back to their houses or fields to look for supplies. Many survived by eating wild berries and roots. Often they did not eat a cooked meal for months at a time. Eventually a great many gave up trying to survive under these circumstances and headed for the cities, where they added their number to the legions of the internally displaced. Many of these interviews were conducted in IDP camps.

♀
Caala
September 2000

My husband and I have always lived in Cuima. It wasn't always easy because you always had to watch out for UNITA attacks, and for FAA offensives. If UNITA attacked one day, then you had to expect the FAA to turn up the day after. Most of the time what happened was that we hid in the bush while UNITA pillaged our houses, and then we stayed there throughout the FAA offensive. Sometimes we stayed more than two weeks in the bush. During those times we lived like animals. We led that life for many years but in 1998 we couldn't continue any longer. That year UNITA's attack surprised us in our houses. My two nephews, who were living with us, tried to escape by evading the UNITA troops but they fell into an ambush on the path they'd taken. Because of their youth they were forced, on pain of death, to join UNITA's

A woman carrying firewood. Caala 2000.

2000 © Atsushi Shibuya

army. Around that time FAA soldiers arrived in the town and gave the order that all of the people must get into their trucks unless they wanted to be killed. So that's what we did. We were several families in FAA trucks that brought us to Caala. That was in March 1998.

So, we've been crammed in here[46] with all of the displaced people who fled from Cuima for more than two years now. (Silence) People are dying like flies because of the living conditions that are imposed on us in this place. We sleep, cook, and eat all one on top of the other. Under these conditions, it's not at all surprising that people die.

This life is especially difficult to accept, considering that in my village I had access to everything. My husband and I had a small piece of land which, when it was well looked after, gave us onions, sweet potatoes and tomatoes. Part of the produce was for our own consumption and part was for sale in the Cuima market, or sometimes in the Caala market. But all of that is behind us today. We must wipe from our minds the notion that one day we will be able to see what we left behind there again. I am sure that those who chased us from our land are waiting for us there to finish off their work. Finish their work means to massacre us. (Silence) Because now the crimes are precise, and they're never left half done. (Laughs) I don't know how wars are fought in other places but here it's not enough to kill. They have to massacre. Like that, even if you survive, you will always carry the mark on you. For those of us who fled Cuima to take refuge with the government, our return home today would be lethal…. We have no intention of going back there now, even though we have always lived there. In this country, once you go over to the other side – even if it's for reasons of survival – you have to expect reprisals.

---

[46] A disused factory serving as a transit centre for IDPs.

I come from Doce. It's a town which has always been under UNITA control, and we always did everything that UNITA told us to do. During each government offensive, UNITA moved away and took all of the population with them. That's a UNITA tactic. With each move we went where they told us to go. In fact they would never leave anyone behind because each person lost was one person more for the government!

But those conditions became more and more difficult and we never saw any of what UNITA promised us. One day, we became afraid that we would be killed by the FAA because we were in a UNITA zone, so we decided to surrender to the FAA. But I took some time to turn myself in to the government because I had always fled from FAA offensives. I always used to go into the bush with the UNITA troops. They basically told us that if we went over to the government we would be killed for coming from a UNITA area. And that's true because during their offensives the FAA wounded or killed everyone who decided not to go with them.

But my family couldn't stand living in the bush any longer, moving every other day so we took advantage of an FAA offensive to surrender. That's how we arrived here in May of this year. We were put in Salsicharia.[47] The whole time I stayed there I was never given a Red Cross ration card. It was very difficult to provide food for all of my family. Every morning I went to look for firewood to sell in the market, and that allowed us to eat a little. I think that the ration card that was meant for me was sold to local people. That is quite common. The officials, who are meant to distribute them, keep them and sell them to locals who have less need than we do. Other than that, diseases spread very rapidly, considering the living conditions in that place. We were all sleeping on top of each

---

[47] A disused factory used to house IDPs.

other, and the latrines didn't work at all. You can imagine the unhygienic conditions that we were living in with no latrines.

When, in July, the administrator came and announced that we would be moved to a new site, out in the open, we were really happy. He also said that in this new site the Red Cross would come and re-register everyone so that we could all receive food.

Now I've been here for almost a month, I can say that as far as sanitation is concerned this place is much better than Salsicharia, but the food situation is worse. Those who had no ration card in Salsicharia, still don't have one. I'm so hungry I can't even finish building my house. I don't understand why the government doesn't put pressure on the Red Cross so that we can all have cards. As I said, today not all of the houses are finished and the sky is already clouded over.[48] If it starts raining we'll really be in a bad way. But I don't know a human being who is capable of working with hunger in his stomach.

I don't know what was the point of my family and me coming over to the government because what we are living through here is exactly the same as the way we used to live when we lived with UNITA. We are robbed, we suffer reprisals for having lived in a UNITA area, and we are hungry. But the FAA also has nothing to eat, so they steal from us. In the end, both sides use the same practices. You can't trust the FAA or UNITA – neither of them. Both sides steal. If you try to argue with them, they shoot at your house. And that's if you're lucky. So now, no matter who's asking, we just hand over what we have.

**Caala
September 2000**

On August 28, 1984, we were taken by UNITA from Catata to a place beyond the Cunene River. We stopped at Chinage. The

---

[48] A sign that the annual rains are about to begin.

populations from about 10 neighbourhoods of Catata were taken there. UNITA took us there to strengthen their logistics, to reinforce their military supply system.

On October 11, 1984, tired of that nomadic life because we were constantly on the move, we decided to come over to the government side. So we fled to Nauaba in Huila Province. There, we were put under surveillance by the military intelligence division. On November 11, 1984, the government troops brought us back to Catata.

In September 1986, we had to flee from UNITA attacks and from government offensives. After nightfall Catata became a real battle field so we took refuge in Caconda, in a place called Dengue. I built a house there which I sold in 1988. We had to leave there because we couldn't manage to feed the children. After that we went to Noioma in the Cuima area. That was in 1988. The Red Cross was present in that area and I benefited from their [food] distribution. I had displaced person's status. After six months the government told us that we had to go back home. So I went back to Catata with my whole family. In my life I have built 18 houses. It's been what you can consider the life of a nomad. Most of those houses were built while I was in UNITA-controlled areas. If you sleep here today, tomorrow you sleep somewhere different. With UNITA we used to build houses every two or three days.

On July 13, 1999, my nephews were killed by UNITA whilst trying to escape. After that, since we weren't safe either with UNITA or with the FAA, we kept on running away from both sides because both the FAA and UNITA threatened and then killed the people who did not agree to go over to their side. They came to look for us in the bush because, in fact, whenever the FAA carried out offensives against Catata we would go and hide in the bush.

We led that life, constantly running away, for five months until we decided to turn ourselves in. It was November 15, 1999, when I reached Caala. There was no more space for my family at Engenharia[49] so we rented a room from some local people in Mangumbala. It was very difficult because we had to pay the rent

---

[49] A disused factory being used as a shelter for IDPs.

and we didn't have any money. But when I heard that at Engenharia a lot of people were dying of disease, because the living conditions were so bad, then I thought that it was better for me and my family to stay in Mangumbala. But it was at a price – all of my children had to work. We went to fetch firewood to sell on the market in Caala. I left the house in Mangumbala on August 11, 1999, which was when we were moved to Cantão [IDP camp]. I'm definitely better off here because I don't have to pay any rent. The whole family still has to work but at least the money that we earn is just for buying food. We go to cut grass to sell to the other displaced people because they need it to make the roofs for their houses.

I would like to be able to go home soon. I had an orange grove there that was more than 250 feet long. It gave me enough money to live. But in March of this year I noticed that the FAA was selling oranges from Catata in the market in Caala. Those are without a doubt my oranges so I think I will have to put up with staying here for a bit longer because I have the impression that the FAA have destroyed my plantation.

♂

Caala
September 2000

I arrived here in December 1998 in a car belonging to the FAA. They had found us on the road when we were running away from UNITA's attacks against Cuima. They said it would be better if they escorted us as far as Caala because the road wasn't safe for people on foot.

The fighting was so violent that I didn't think twice before getting in that car. I had left behind a town which had been turned into an abattoir. I stank of blood and death. So when the FAA came along we felt safer but it wasn't easy to get into their car. But still…you know at a moment like that it's better not to think too much because a bullet travels fast. Perhaps if I'd have been on my own I wouldn't have got into the car. But I was there with all of my family and my children are still small.

We arrived in Caala with nothing in our hands because we didn't have the time to take anything at all – only the clothes that we were wearing. In Caala we were welcomed by the Sisters who looked after us for a time. They gave us three kilograms of maize and a glass of salt every two weeks. But that didn't last very long. Little by little, the number of displaced people increased and the ration wasn't enough to feed everyone. That's when my family and I moved to the [derelict] railway station with all the other displaced people who had run away from Cuima. That was in December 1998.

We've been here for almost two years, and in those two years my life has stopped. I have ended up wondering if I did the right thing in coming here. It's important to ask myself that question because if one day I want to go back to Cuima or to an area controlled by UNITA I won't be able to because I will be considered a traitor. It's a pity for me that all of my fields are today in an area controlled by UNITA. I should have thought a bit longer before coming here but war forces you to take quick decisions. Today I can't tell which would have been better for my family – to live with the anguish of being killed, burnt, or massacred but to be at home with your plate full or to benefit from the protection of the FAA but to die of hunger or disease. Because here we are all dependent on humanitarian aid, if the "whites" don't feed us we sleep with hunger in our bellies. In Cuima all of my family worked in the fields. We grew maize and sweet potatoes. Here we don't have any land to cultivate because you need money to buy some. Just imagine if I was able to buy some land, then afterwards I would also have to buy some seed.... With no money the problem remains the same, in other words unsolvable. That's why, when the administrator told us that the government wanted us to go back to Cuima, I was pretty happy. If the whole community went back we would be protected by our numbers. But I'm scared that I won't be able to cultivate my land any more because normally, when the soldiers occupy a town, they put mines everywhere so that the people cannot go back there. That's what must have happened in Cuima so it's likely that a lot of people will be mutilated before we can resettle there. In fact the more I think about going back there, the more I think that now is not the right time. And that attack which took place last week is proof. I get the feeling that the government thinks that we don't know what goes on there (laughs, bitterly).

In fact, I think that life becomes more risky when you have, like me, lived in areas occupied successively by UNITA and the MPLA. The reprisals are equally cruel from one side or the other. Personally I do and I don't want to go back to Cuima. I do because I grew up there and I left all of my things there but I couldn't bear to see what I've seen in Cuima again. I saw war there; I saw the most barbaric kind of death – with a machete. I have a cousin who was kidnapped and taken by force into the bush by UNITA. UNITA threatened to cut him up if he didn't obey their orders. To this day I don't know what fate will have been awaiting him there. Two of my sisters were also taken to be what they call "married." I've never seen them again. (Silence)....on the other hand FAA offensives are also frightening because their methods are almost identical. It's good that they brought us here but we are, and always will be, treated like traitors because we supported UNITA even if it was just for a short time.

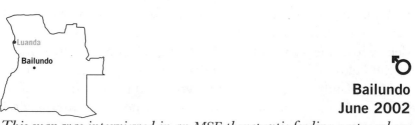

Bailundo
June 2002

This man was interviewed in an MSF therapeutic feeding centre where one of his daughters was being treated. Another of his children had died of measles three weeks before the interview.

I live in Caimba where a lot of the children have measles. Sixteen children died in April and May and another four have died since the beginning of June. The people don't have any transport to get to the hospital in Bailundo to get their children vaccinated.

Caimba was under government control until 1992. At that time the population started moving back there, after the peace accords, but a few months later the war flared up again and UNITA took the village. They controlled it until 1999.

In 1999, when the FAA captured Bailundo, the situation got complicated in Caimba. The population were forced to run away into the bush with UNITA troops. We stayed there for 20 days. During that time there was a disagreement between UNITA soldiers – some wanted to let the civilians go back home, and others wanted to keep them in the bush. But the FAA started to threaten our position and UNITA leaders decided to let the civilians go so that they wouldn't slow down the escape of the soldiers. So then we decided to go back to Caimba. From then on the village was never calm again. The FAA came to Caimba regularly to enforce their control over us, and they pillaged, and raped, and burnt the houses. The women had to hide every time the FAA arrived. We villagers were forced to give our harvests to the government soldiers, and to transport them to an FAA military base several hours walk away. I know one person who died from exhaustion carrying that food for the FAA. For their part, UNITA kept on coming to the village to

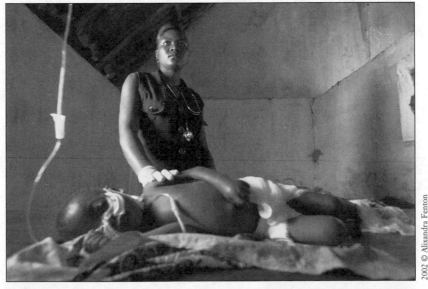

2002 © Alixandra Fenton

A local pediactrics nurse watches over a sick child recovering in the temporary ward of Bailundo Government hospital. Sick as a result of malnutrition, the child is being cared for by an MSF team. Bailundo 2002.

steal – especially salt – and also to burn some houses during the night. We only had sweet potatoes left to eat. It was only in April 2002 that, in terms of security, things started to get better. My family has nothing left, except the clothes we have on us.

Cuito
May 2000

The ones that remained [in the village after the attack of March 1999] found themselves between the *batidas*[50] of government troops and UNITA attacks in which they robbed, recruited young men by force and killed civilians. At first, UNITA came after the *sobas*, the civil servants, the catechists and the families that had kids in the army. When they'd find the *sobas* they would force them to denounce those people or they'd be killed. As for the people, UNITA also forced them into labour such as transporting heavy tree trunks to build bridges over the Rivers Cunje, Colongue and Sanga. If they couldn't take it they'd be shot…. As for the government troops, they also looted civilians' homes as well as government structures, and they demanded that the population denounce those that had UNITA in their families. If the population refused to speak, they'd be beaten. FAA soldiers also raped women.

Lombe
December 2000

I was a school teacher in Calandula. In Malange, I did a training

---

[50] Operations where FAA troops steal civilians' possessions and then force the civilians to transport them to FAA bases.

course to improve my teaching skills. During that time, I was paid 19 kwanzas[51] a month, but not every month. In March, once I finished the course and was qualified, I received 100 kwanzas a month. My wife still had to make and sell charcoal for extra money.

I was told by the Ministry of Education to come to this village of Lombe and that I would receive food from the WFP[52] for working as a school teacher. The first month I received food but WFP came and changed the registration during a time when I was in Malange and my name was removed from the list. Since then I have not received any food. I went to the Ministry of Education and they told me that the people of the village should give me food because they want a teacher here. In the end, I have not been paid a salary for five months.

In October 1998, there was a big UNITA attack in Calandula. It was a combat attack with the FAA who were in the town but many of the civilian population in the surrounding neighbourhoods were also killed. Children, women, everyone UNITA saw – because they were there living with the government. Realising I could not stay in my house, I tried to flee to the bush with my family but we were caught by UNITA. We were taken to a house and forced inside to be burnt together. Some people were afraid to go inside, once they realised the intentions of UNITA, and were beaten and shot. There were many people inside the house but we managed to loosen and remove one of the mud bricks, from where we escaped one by one.

I fled directly to the bush with my family and headed to Malange. It took four days to reach Malange, one of which was spent wading through a river waist-high with the children on our backs and carrying others. In Malange, I rented a house in a neighbourhood with many other family members.

From 1975 to about 1981 or 1982, Calandula was controlled by the government. From about 1982, UNITA used to come and attack and retreat back into the bush. In 1992, after the elections, UNITA came and the FAA ran away. This was a particularly bad time for the people as UNITA was blaming them for losing the elections and the population was made to suffer [in reprisal]. UNITA would come and find the *sobas* of the neighbourhoods and

---

[51] Angolan currency.
[52] The UN World Food Programme.

kill them because it was their fault the population had voted for the MPLA. They had supported the MPLA and now the MPLA had fled so the population would have to pay. The people were not allowed to listen to the radio or speak badly of UNITA. Those who did would be found and killed. The population was told that they had to change their minds and belong to UNITA. The young men were taken to fight for UNITA and the younger girls and boys taken for JURA. JURA was a group that was made to sing and dance for the soldiers. The girls were also there for the soldiers to use for sex. The soldiers could pick and choose as they liked. Even when they left their base to go to other locations, the group from JURA was taken with them and made to carry the ammunition.

In 1995 or 1996, a government administration was put in place but UNITA still remained living with the people. In 1997, the UN was sent to ask UNITA for a cease-fire. It was also announced on the radio that the FAA was coming and requesting UNITA not to fight. The population was told that they must not support the FAA but many of FAA soldiers had family in Calandula who were very happy when they arrived. The FAA came and UNITA left to the bush without fighting. Shortly afterwards UNITA reorganised themselves in the bush and began to attack. With the first big attack, all the population fled to the bush. During the second attack, the FAA left and UNITA took control of Calandula for 24 hours.

I was recruited by FAPLA in 1979 but in 1981 I was shot in two places in my arm and was sent to the hospital in Luanda. For the next five years I couldn't work. In 1987, I began teaching again, as I did before I was recruited. When UNITA came in 1992 I continued to work since a teacher as I was injured and could not fight for them.

Cuito
May 2000

On February 19 [2000], myself and a large group of people left

Belo Horizonte early in the morning to go and collect food in our fields. When we got there each person went to his own field. Around midday, I was filling bags of beans when I saw five soldiers coming closer. I thought they were government troops

Landmine victims. Luena 2001.

2001 © Joanna Ladomirska

doing their patrolling and that's why I didn't run away but in fact they were UNITA troops. They came closer to me and started beating me up with wooden sticks. Then they tied me up with ropes and one soldier said that they were going to kill me. Another soldier then said that they were not going to kill me. He said that they had warned us that if the government came we should not leave to Belo Horizonte. His words were, "So we are going to cut off your ears because you are deaf. If you could hear well you wouldn't have gone to Belo Horizonte knowing that it is with the government."

In fact, it's true that after they lost Andulo they started warning us that if the government took Belo Horizonte no one could leave to go to the town, and that the ones who would go to stay with the government could not come back to their fields. But until this happened to me, no one really thought that they would go so far. We didn't really think that they'd do more than beat us up. So, they didn't beat me too much because they knew that the government had been patrolling the area. They tied me up around my feet, my knees and around my wrists too. They put me on my knees and put my hands on a tree branch that was lying on the floor. They separated my hands and one soldier hit me five times with a machete on my right forearm and it fell on the floor. No one held me and I did not resist either. They told me to stand up, and the same guy cut my right ear off and threw it on the ground. It was just one straight cut because the knife was very sharp. Then they told me to leave, to go away and show it to the others in Belo Horizonte.

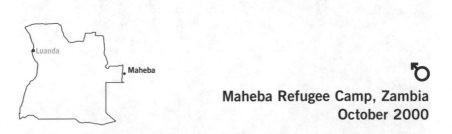

Maheba Refugee Camp, Zambia
October 2000

The war started in 1983. We lived for three years with UNITA, then UNITA left Cazombo and the MPLA controlled the town until 1995; then from 1995 UNITA came back. In 1999, the war started up again. UNITA took a lot of the young people, all of them, for compulsory military service and fighting. Many ran away to Zambia a long time ago and are here in Maheba because they didn't want to be recruited and be forced to fight.

In May [2000], the war started on the 12th, the MPLA bombed the buildings and groups of FAA soldiers attacked the surrounding villages to steal, take the bicycles, the clothes, the animals. They killed a lot of young people between the age of 15 and 18. I saw them killing them myself. The MPLA said they were from UNITA. It wasn't true. In July, that started up again because the planes started bombing again. The people started running away towards Cavungo, others ran towards Lumbala Caquengue, towards Zambezi.

I left for Cavungo. I stayed there during July, August and September. Then the war started again in Camafoafa and came to Cavungo. On September 24, the war entered Cavungo. On the 26th the *soba* of the village set off with the whole population to go to Zambia, in the direction of Luau Mission. When we got to Lovua there were UNITA soldiers who didn't want us to go to Zambia. They started beating us. Then the planes started bombing Lovua and UNITA soldiers ran away, so we were able to carry on, on our way to Zambia. In Lovua there was a lieutenant colonel from UNITA who wanted the civilians to stay behind with them, and some people were taken by force to go into the forest with them. Other civilians were captured by MPLA soldiers and taken back to Cavungo. Between Lovua and Luau Mission we didn't have any problems. We walked at night on the way there. We were afraid of both UNITA and MPLA bombs.

If the war finished for good I would go back to Angola. Otherwise I will stay here. In Angola we used to have so many problems. Since 1992 I used to trade fish for salt and soap in Zambia. We had to pay 5000 kwachas[53] to get a *laissez-passer* from UNITA to allow us to go and sell things in Zambia. The girls aged between 12 and 25 were taken away to make food, sing and dance for UNITA soldiers, even the married women. My own daughter was taken when she was 12. They kept her until she was 14 and

---

[53] Zambian currency.

then she ran away. Fortunately she was protected by a *soba* and UNITA could not take her back again. She was lucky, thank God. Me, I was forced to transport weapons for 80 kilometres, and so were my children, from 1983 until 1992 and even until now, many times. My 20-year-old son was taken for compulsory military service, and later on they appointed him youth leader for sport but he refused because didn't want to force the other young people into training. He refused, so they whipped him and put him in prison in 1998 for one year.

Mayukwayukwa Refugee Camp, Zambia
March 2001

I was born in Angola, near Lumbala N'guimbo, in 1960, but my parents brought me to live in Zambia while I was still a child. The nationalist movements started fighting against the Portuguese and there was trouble in our area so they decided to become refugees. I grew up in Senanga; my father worked as a mechanic. I went to school there, which is why I speak English. I don't know any Portuguese. I lived in Zambia until 1991, life was normal. But in 1991 there was peace in Angola, and I decided to go back there. My parents had both died, but I had an uncle still living in Lumbala N'guimbo who I'd never met, so I decided to go and live with him. I wanted to see what my country looked like.

For the first couple of years, life in Angola was fine, it was good. Lumbala was controlled by UNITA, but it was peacetime and they didn't make any trouble. But then the war started again, after the elections, and UNITA became very bad. They were always controlling the people, forcing the people to work for them, taking their food and treating them really badly. I got fed up with them and wanted to come back to live in Zambia. But my uncle said, "No, you must not leave. If you leave, then UNITA will kill me to punish me for letting you escape." So I had to stay.

UNITA did not want any of the people to leave because they used them like slaves. They took me several times to carry their weapons. They would come to the village and force us to leave with them to the places where they had their weapons hidden in the bush. They would give us heavy loads of bombs and ammunition to carry, and force us to walk very far to deliver those things to the front lines. Sometimes we had to walk for four or six weeks, just to get to the front lines, and then we had to walk all the way back again. We had to carry all of our own food and water as well as their equipment. If you did not have food then you would just starve. Many people were bitten by snakes or were too weak to survive those journeys. UNITA would just leave them behind in the bush, to be eaten by the lions. You could not refuse to work for them. I tried once. They caught me and tied my arms like this (holds his arms behind his back, showing how his elbows and wrists were tied together) and beat me with a stick. Then they put me in a hole in the ground, in the dark, still with my arms tied, and left me there for some days. After that I didn't resist any more. We lived like that from 1992 until 1999.

In 2000, the MPLA attacked Lumbala N'guimbo and UNITA ran away to hide in their bases in the bush. The FAA came to our

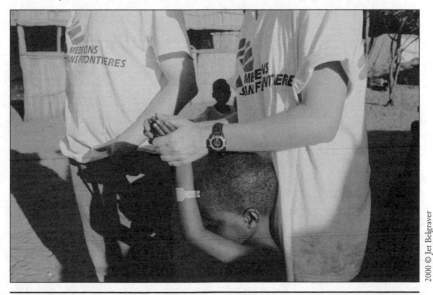

2000 © Jet Belgraver

Over 3000 Angolan refugees fled across the border to Sillilimwe refugee camp set up by MSF in Kalabo, Zambia. Kalabo 2000.

village and they called all of the men to a meeting in Lumbala N'guimbo. They told us that we must all join the Civil Defence, then they gave us guns and bullets, but no training. Then they sent us back to our villages and told us we must go into the bush to find UNITA and fight them. We did that, we fought with UNITA and they ran away. But then a few days later they came back to our village and killed many people. They were saying things like, "You stayed with us for such a long time but when the MPLA came you went to work for them, so now we will kill you." Luckily I was away in the forest when they came. We went back to the FAA and asked them to come and fight UNITA, but they refused. Then, a short while later, UNITA launched a big attack and captured Lumbala back from the FAA. The FAA all ran away and they told the people, "Now you must run away to Zambia because UNITA are coming and we cannot protect you." We were angry with the FAA, but we all ran to Zambia. We had to walk for two weeks through the bush to get across the border. UNITA had patrols on the paths trying to catch people who were running away, so we had to walk through the deep bush, hiding in the day and walking at night. Once we were in Zambia we came first to Kalabo, then to Mongu, then to this camp. I do not want to go back to Angola again. Even if there is peace, I will stay here in Zambia.

Matala
February 2001

Five of my children died there in Chipindo because there were no hospitals or medicines. They were all very small. They were sick because their mother had the sickness inside her and there were no medicines to cure her. I have two children here with me and my wife is pregnant again. We left our village in a group of 30 people. By the time we reached Kuvango there were 36 people. We arrived there on January 8, 2001. Some people continued to

Matala but I stayed, with 16 other people, to wait for documentation. Whilst we were there we were given food and then we were brought by car to Matala. When we arrived in Matala we were given tents, food, tools and four cows. We have a communal field but it is small. We had a meeting with the *sobas* and the government today to ask for more land. We also need seeds. Here we have a health post in this tent, and there, in that tent, we will make a school. But we don't want to stay here; we want to move closer to Matala. We told them this in the meeting today. We have just come out of the bush, and now they have put us back in the bush again. Here there are no police, no FAA, just us with no weapons. We don't have any arms here, nothing to defend ourselves with. If UNITA comes here, that is the end of us, we will all die. And UNITA knows where we have gone. They always know. If they want they can find us here.

I was with FAPLA for 10 years, from 1978 to 1988 (he shows a number tattooed on his forearm). Yes, UNITA saw this, but I told them it was from when I was fighting for UNITA in the old days and they believed me (laughs hard). I am from Bié but since the time I left with FAPLA I have never returned. After that I moved to Jamba[54] from 1989 to 1996. In 1997, there was a sort of peace and I moved to Chipindo. I went to live in N′gola but there I found that there was no peace. UNITA was not allowing the people to leave the village; they threatened to kill us if we did. So since that time I have been trapped there. We suffered there, like the cows suffer when they are ploughing the fields (laughs). UNITA would take the food from the people and make them suffer a lot. It wasn't like that when I was with FAPLA, we were given food or bought our own. Things have changed now, even the way of the FAA has changed. One day some FAA came to the village. They went to the house of some people and took the women and children, and took them to Jamba. But they took all the men from the house, four men and even the nine-year-old boy, and shot them all. And those men were just farmers there, living on the side of UNITA because they had no choice, those men didn't know anything about UNITA but the FAA killed them all the same. Some people there wanted to go with the FAA but when the FAA

---

[54] The town in Huila Province, not UNITA's headquarters in Cuando Cubango.

arrived the people just ran to the bush because they were afraid that they would be killed too. UNITA used to come to the village and have meetings with the people. They'd tell the people that everyone on the MPLA side is hungry and that they have no fields. The people believe them and stay there. They told us, "The president of the United States, Bill Clinton, is going to send us arms, so that we can finish this war." You have to believe what they tell you otherwise they kill you.

⚦

Cangandala
November 2000

I arrived in Cangandala just two days ago and I'm living in a transit house [for IDPs] while I wait to be registered and moved to a neighbourhood. Our group living in the transit centre has received some food from the administrator of Cangandala for a couple of days. I came with nine people from my village, we walked freely to Zonga. It took about one day. In Zonga, we were joined by about another 100 people from there. We fled during the night and it took five days to reach Cangandala. No one brought anything with them because we had nothing to bring. We brought some maize but it was taken by FAA troops when we arrived in Sungui.

Since 1992, Cahumbi was under UNITA. There I had to build houses for UNITA, transport goods and work in the fields. The women also had to work in the fields and prepare cassava flour for the soldiers. There was no school or health post, only a church. There was a lot of sickness that we would treat by boiling roots and drinking the water. In September 1999, the FAA arrived and told us to go to Dumba Kabango [12 kilometres away], where we would be protected by the FAA. After many people had left, UNITA put up check-points to stop the people going to the government side. The only people that remained in the villages were those forced to by UNITA. In Dumba Kabango there were 48 sobas, representing different villages, and possibly up to 6,000 or 7,000 people. There, the people built grass huts and worked for the residents and got paid in maize. We also exchanged clothes and other items for food. The living conditions were very poor and overcrowded. The water from the wells was not good for drinking. There was no health post but one time some government workers came from Cambundi Catembo and vaccinated the children for tetanus and measles. The FAA left the area before Christmas 1999 and went back to Cambundi Catembo. The people were left behind, exposed to UNITA. When the FAA was there, they would ask us for food. Giving them food was neither voluntary nor obligatory. Once the FAA left, UNITA would come and take our food, possessions and children. We were suffering a lot there from UNITA. Life was worse there than it had been in our home area.

In April 2000, there was a big attack by UNITA, there was a lot of fighting. The FAA came and chased UNITA away. In May, there was another attack on the people in Dumba Kabango and some people were killed. The FAA was not present. After that second attack the FAA told all the people to return to their home areas. Initially the people had been very happy that the FAA had told them to move to Dumba Kabango as they would be protected and they had had enough of suffering because of UNITA. After the FAA abandoned them in December, and then told the people to return to their home area in May, the people were not happy with the FAA. It took me two or three days to return home through the bush with my family. My house was still there but all our belongings in the house were gone, except for those things that we hid in the bush before we left. UNITA followed the people back to the villages and were very cross with the people because we had gone and lived on the government side. UNITA was worse than ever, so the people had to leave once again and come to Cangandala. Only the old people stayed behind in the villages.

♀
Two women
Matala
February 2001

We left our village in search of food. We were not going to our fields; we were looking for cassava about 16 kilometres away. We would go to that place and back in the same day. We were a group of seven women and two men. While we were there, the FAA found us and asked us what we were doing, they told us that we could not stay there. They captured us and brought us to Matala. It took us two days; one night we slept in a village on the way. We have been here two weeks.

We are here alone, with only the children that we were carrying on our backs. Our husbands and all our other children are still there in our village. We have had no contact with them. We are worried because our children are small and now we can't go back. We can't go back because if we do UNITA will kill us because we came here with the FAA. And they [the women's families] can't leave because UNITA is there. They can only come here if the FAA goes there to get them. Now we don't know what to do. We are happy we are here because here we have salt and they gave us food and other things, but we have no family here.

I don't know if I will see my children again. If God helps, one day I will see my children again.

⚲
Cangandala
December 2000

There were no health posts anywhere, not even in Luquembo or

Cambundi Catembo. There were only traditional medicines. There were never vaccinations. I had four fields; they produced enough food for my family - peanuts, beans, cassava. For extra money, I would fish in the River Roando and trade fish for salt, clothes and soap in Caculama. That was only possible in the past, during peace. Here, I have a ration card, and make charcoal for extra income. I have received land, a hoe and seeds just recently. I have enough for the family. I live in Boa Chegada [IDP camp] with my family. I arrived here just before Christmas 1999. It was a four day walk, with the FAA as an escort. Everyone from the village came. We encountered no problems on the road. Unfortunately, I brought absolutely nothing because we were forced to flee immediately. When the FAA came there was no time. The troops appeared to be fearful that UNITA would return so they wanted us to leave in a hurry. FAA troops told the people that they would leave, and when UNITA returned the people would be killed. The FAA also told us that anyone who chose to stay was a UNITA supporter. Nobody stayed.

UNITA had been holding the village since 1997. When the FAA started to have victories and advancing on the area, UNITA started killing people – mostly young men. They killed them with knives and with guns. UNITA said that they were killing the young men because they would end up joining the FAA and fighting against them. UNITA was going from village to village, looking for people. Everybody fled into the bush. You had to take your whole family or UNITA would torture your wife and children to make them say where you were. I fled to the bush more times than I could count. In the bush, we had small houses, near our fields, where we would stay for days, or even a week or two. Under UNITA there was no trade at all. No soap, salt or clothes. UNITA believed that if people were permitted to go to town for trading, they would tell the FAA where to come and find the rebels. UNITA made a school but the children could not learn because they used bamboo leaves for paper and charcoal for writing. Everybody in the village had to give UNITA cassava flour and goats too. Depending on the size of your household, it worked out to between 14 and 30 plates of flour per family per week. If the village did not meet its quota, the *soba* would be beaten with a tree branch 150 times. I cannot go back because of UNITA. Even if there is peace, I will stay in Cangandala. I am happy here and charcoal gives me enough money to buy things.

🜨

Bunjei
May 2002

Bunjei was one of a number of towns where the FAA brought the civilians they had rounded up in the bush during their scorched earth campaign. Once there, the civilian population quickly ran out of food. Humanitarian agencies could not gain access to Bunjei until the war ended. It is estimated that, as a result, over 1,000 people, or 8 percent of the population of Bunjei starved to death in the last six months of the war.

At night we listen to the radio because there isn't much to do. We listen to music, the news…. We also listen to the hours go by so we don't have to think about this suffering, the suffering that

People travelling from Bunjei to Caala. Threatened by attacks from UNITA, they were unable to move until the cease-fire. Bunjei 2002.

we've lived through. In January and February, at this time of night, the people were weeping. Throughout Bunjei you could only hear people crying – crying for the children, for the women, for the old people who had died that day. And all of us – every one of us – when we heard that weeping at night thought, "Maybe tomorrow it will be for us…. They will be weeping for us." We never knew if we would be here the next day to see the sun rise because we had nothing. When the women wept for their dead children, they were also weeping for their own loneliness because they were left on their own. They couldn't advance or retreat; they couldn't go anywhere at all unless they died. They thought, "What will become of me?" The mothers didn't have the strength to pick up their dead children or to dig their graves because at that time each person had to dig the graves for their own dead. Nobody had the strength to help the others. Today the women are like men, there are no women expecting children now because they don't have the strength to make love. When we used to leave Bunjei to go and look for cassava to eat, UNITA would let us pass on our way out, but when we were on the way back, with one or two kilograms of cassava, they would cut off our heads with machetes. When we saw that someone had gone out one or two days before and still not come back, then we knew that they were dead. There were some people who still had the strength to go and fetch their dead, so that they wouldn't be left in the bush, and there were others who didn't have the strength. Sometimes – when there was some – we ate cassava flour with no salt or oil but on the next day things would be even worse. People would get bloody diarrhoea that wouldn't stop and then they'd die.

I am 48 years old and I've lost six children, while I was in the bush. Only one of my children is alive today.[55] In the bush our children were allowed to stay with us until they reached 12 years old, after that they belonged to UNITA. They became the slaves of the commanders and the soldiers. Because UNITA soldiers who came to attack the villages used to make the children walk in front of them. That way, they cleared the route – if there were mines, bombs, animals or snakes…the children cleared the way. Sometimes UNITA soldiers from the north would come here to

---

[55] His child was severely malnourished and in an MSF feeding centre.

fetch children. Then we knew that we had no hope of ever seeing them again. The parents couldn't say anything, otherwise they were considered to be undisciplined agitators. And agitators get their heads cut off. There, in the bush, they didn't really like killing the people with bullets. It was a waste. They preferred to use a machete or a bush knife. One day one old man went to the fields to look for cassava. They let him go. But when he was coming back they caught him, confiscated his harvest and said, "We will not kill you because you are old." So they cut off his ear and forced him to eat it, saying that it was bread. Along the edge of the river they had laid mines, so that we couldn't go and fetch water without them. If anyone found a way to go to the river and come back without triggering a mine, then the next day the soldiers would see their footprints. They wouldn't rub out the footprints, but they would put mines on the new path. The girls who were about 12 or 13 were forced to join JURA. The girls also had to mobilise the children, and carry the weapons. When they attacked villages the girls carried the weapons and the boys went to pillage the houses, each one accompanied by a soldier, while the other soldiers shot at the people. The boys who pillaged never got to keep any of the loot, the soldiers kept everything. Whenever the government attacked it was the same thing. We didn't know where to go; it was the same thing from one side and from the other. Now we prefer to be here, where we can sleep easy. If they manage to do the demobilisation properly, maybe the people will be free.

There are still a lot of people in the bush who have to come here. Even here in this village there are UNITA soldiers. The ones here didn't do much harm, there's no point in them turning themselves in. They were just obeying orders, and the people know that but a few weeks ago, a young man, 22 years old, arrived here to hand himself in to the government. The people here almost killed him because he was one of the terrors of UNITA. It was the [FAA] soldiers who saved him. He had no respect at all for others; he could kill five or six people in a row with a machete. Why he did that we don't know. He also wanted to kill his own father. How is it possible for someone to get like that, to the point of wanting to kill his own father, who is like a God for us? That's really the madness of men. Today we can see a woman with a child in her arms, and she looks so old, so worn out, that she looks like the child's grandmother. But in fact she's only 18 and she's the child's mother but she's devastated by suffering. Now they're asking us to forget all of that. Maybe the children will be able to, but us, the old people, we are of an age to have grandchildren and we don't even have any children who can give us grandchildren. We have seen hundreds of people being massacred and, for a long time, we could say nothing. We have spent years between life and death. And now, is it possible to live with the people who did all that? We won't be able to forget. These white people [MSF] have really done a good job because at this time of night, a little over a month ago, we could only hear crying and more crying. I arrived here in November, brought by the government [who burnt his village]. I don't know if one day we will have everything we used to have again. We have to start again from zero. And even then...you see that house (points at the ruins of a house) it belonged to a man who used to have 100 cows and lots of land. Today he lives in a shack, like everyone else in Bunjei. In the olden days Bunjei was a garden where fruit grew without anyone tending it. The inhabitants used to stay here six months of the year, picking fruit and selling it. And then they had enough money to travel around the country for the other six months of the year.

♀
Caala
May 2002

This woman had been transported to Caala from Bunjei so her children could be treated in an MSF feeding centre.

We suffered a lot. We had nothing to make the children better, no salt, no clothes, no soap, and nothing to eat. We never stayed in one place. Sometimes we could stay for two days in the same place but afterwards, we had to move on again. Sometimes it was every day, we'd walk 10 kilometres and then walk back again. One day we chose one of the two sides. We were already tired of being attacked by UNITA and by the MPLA, so we decided to go and live with the government in Bunjei. But there also, there was no food. There was a lady who sold salt and other things but as we had no money we continued to have nothing. In the beginning we used to go and look for cassava and sweet potatoes. Later on there was no more cassava, there was nothing, and then the sickness began. I have three children. Two are here and my 14-year-old daughter stayed in Bunjei. I was born in Chipeta in Bié Province. When I was 10 years old I was taken to a military base. My father had died in the war, and my mother had died of a disease. That's what I was told because I never knew them. It was my oldest brother who brought me up. I was 10 when my brother and I were attacked by UNITA while we were on our way to the fields. They took me to a base and from then on I moved constantly from base to base. We stayed in bases or in some other place in the forest. That was the war. In the beginning, since I was little, I didn't have anything particular to do. There were a lot of children, and the older children looked after us. They made a *jango*[56] for the children. There was no mother to look after us, just the older children. Later on we had to clean the houses and the clothes, cook, prepare the flour.... We did everything.

When I was 15 I got married to a soldier. I had a son soon afterwards and we had a hut for ourselves. We were in Mavinga, then in Bié and in Andulo – always in military bases. Every two months we would move to another base. We also used to go to the villages and each house had to give us a plate of maize or something else. I used to go with the soldiers and bring back the food, I would carry whatever we had managed to get. From Andulo we went to Bailundo and then to Base 21. Then in 1992, when there was peace, we went to a demobilisation camp for the soldiers. When the war started again I went to Huíla, to the base at Cope. I was always with my husband. At that time, in 1994, I had five children. Afterwards, with the war, we were always moving from base to base, until 2000. My husband died in a battle with the FAA. And then the commander of our troops killed two of my children, aged four and five, in front of

---

[56] A large, round, thatched shelter.

me. It was to give him strength – by killing the children he would gain powers…. He killed them in front of me, with a bullet. That was in Matombé. When my husband died I was already pregnant with the last child. So, after that, I ran away from the base and went to a village in Chissende, in Huila. I fled with my three surviving children. That was at the end of 2000. I was well received by the people in the village, I worked for them in their fields and in return they gave me food. We were only short of salt, soap and clothes, but apart from that everything was fine. UNITA soldiers didn't give us much trouble because we used to work a lot and every family gave them 100 kilograms of maize [per month]. Those who couldn't give it were killed because UNITA said they were useless. I saw three people being killed for that. The villagers used to give me five kilograms of maize for each day I worked, and I only had to give 50 kilograms to UNITA because I was a widow. The MPLA also attacked us frequently, they used to arrive and we would run away. They would steal everything they could and then we would go back when they had gone away again. It was like that for the whole of 2001. Later on there was a lot of confusion. We were always running away from the MPLA and from UNITA who both used to attack us constantly. In the end we decided to abandon UNITA and the whole village went to an MPLA area.

There was an attack and we decided to hand ourselves over to FAA soldiers and leave with them. That was in June 2001. We went to Bunjei. There, we used to go out to look for food – we would walk three days and then go back again. I was there with my three children who are 11, six and 18 months. In Bunjei there was nothing to eat, no clothes, no salt but we were well treated. They defended us from UNITA when we went to the fields. I came here [to Caala] one and a half months ago in the MSF truck, just with my youngest child who was sick. I left the other two in Bunjei. Afterwards the doctors brought the six year old here too because he had also become sick. He was in the intensive care section and I saw him arrive. Now he's already better and he's back with me. The little one is also better. When we got here he only weighed two kilograms and now he weighs six. He's almost ready to be discharged. I didn't bring the other children when I came because they had to stay there to guard our house.

♀
Chipindo
August 2002

I was born and raised in Cuvango. In 1982, I finished my training
to be a teacher. After the elections in 1992, UNITA captured
Cuvango and people who lived there, like myself, could not leave.
At that time I was married and had three children. My house was
occupied and we had to give them everything we had. My husband escaped and I haven't seen him since. My children stayed
with me. When UNITA occupies a house and there is a woman
there, she has to marry a UNITA man in order not to think about
the man from the other party [MPLA]. So I then married another
man, a man from UNITA, but he was not a soldier, he worked in
agriculture. In the bush I had another three children. First I
worked for UNITA as a teacher and then they chose me as a leader
for their women's organisation. In 1993, when UNITA left, they
took everyone with them to the bush. I spent almost 10 years in
the same area; first in Canjivale, then in Kilometre 50, then
beyond the Nbale River. In 1996, I went alone to Bailundo for
three months with one of my children for a course on political
training. Then I went back to Canjivale and lived there for a
while. I used to go often to Kilometre 50 because my husband
lived there. The distance between the two was 30 kilometres and
I did that around five times a year.

In Canjivale we had a collective field where we produced food
for the troops and for Kilometre 50. Kilometre 50 was an administrative position that belonged to Cuvango Municipality. There
were around 5,000 people who lived in the area of Kilometre 50,
up to Quimbale River, but most of them have died or gone else-
where recently because there were no UNITA forces left to defend
them. I stayed in Canjivale between 1993 and 2001. In January
2000, an intense war started in that area. There were frequent
attacks, every 15 or 30 days, and people were killed with bullets,

with machetes, with knives. These attacks were different from the ones in the past when people did not die so much. Recently, since November 2001, people were dying more because of machetes and

This undernourished child waits to be admitted to the MSF feeding centre in Chipindo. Chipindo 2002.

knives. The killing stopped only in March 2002. In November [2001], they [FAA] would come to a village, collect the people and burn the houses. Sometimes they'd also kill people because they were wasting time in the bush instead of turning themselves in to the government. In Canjivale, in 2000, there were six attacks by the FAA. We would run away to the bush and they'd burn our houses. Then we would come back and rebuild. By the end of 2000 the UNITA bases started to move around. In January 2001, my husband was put in prison in UNITA's Cope base, beyond the Kwengue River. He was taken because he had been with the MPLA before. When my husband was released from prison we remained in the Cope area. Cope was the largest base in Huila and lately it did not have a fixed location any more – we moved a lot. We moved every time we were attacked but we remained the whole time in the area of the rivers in Galangue. When we were caught we were in the area between Chinguinde and Chinoca.

By the time we were caught we had no cattle left. When we lived in Canjivale we had a lot of food and a large variety as well. When we were in Cope we ate cassava, sweet potato and maize from time to time. At that time we still had cattle but every time they [FAA] attacked us they'd take a few. The collective fields finished in the end of 2000. After that, each family looked after its own food. With the constant attacks, we would run away and leave the food behind. Sometimes we'd spend two days without any food. I was caught on December 21, 2001, by FAA troops from Bunjei. When I was caught, there had already been many attacks. I was at home preparing food, around five in the afternoon, when we heard shooting. I grabbed my children and ran away to the bush. I was pregnant. My husband was in another base working in the fields. For one day I was alone with my children before other people showed up. We then went back to the village and saw that everything had been destroyed and the houses had been burnt. Seven women and three children lay dead on the ground. They had been shot dead from the back. They were not from my village but I knew them. They were cultivating some fields close to our village. They live beyond Cutato River. They had probably been brought to the village by FAA soldiers on their way. So we went back into the bush, to Chinoca. The next day, we were having a rest when they caught us. It was almost six in the morning. There were 12 soldiers in their group. We knew they were coming and we were already running away from them. When they found us they told us not to run away otherwise they would kill us. They took everything we had, told us to undress and took our clothes as well. They took us with them and on the way, three women – one young one and two older ones – were raped. The soldiers came and chose the women they wanted. The younger one was 15 years old. She was crying and she did not want to go with them. They started shooting near her legs until she agreed to follow them. She was raped by one man and was allowed to join our group afterwards. The only women who were not raped were those who were pregnant. There was one man in the group. He was around 50 years old. He was beaten up and his arms were tied. Then they gave him a 50-kilogram bag of maize to carry. Even myself, pregnant, they gave me a 30-kilogram bag to carry. We took two days to get to Bunjei. When we got to Bunjei, the young girl and another woman were "married" to soldiers. In Bunjei we were well received and they did not do us any harm. I met people there from my family, from Cuvango, whom I hadn't seen since 1993. In Bunjei there was no food. Some people were running away to the bush again, to find their children. If the FAA found them again, they were killed. In Bunjei there was a small market and there were traders coming from Caala. Some people would work in exchange for food. I was working carrying cassava and cutting firewood in exchange for one kilogram of flour. In Bunjei there was some food coming from the government but it was very, very little, like one cup of flour per person. In January 2002, my son was born and in February my sister's husband showed up and took me to Lubango because my family there was looking for me. I stayed there for two months, until March 28 when I went to Matala to see my mum, whom I hadn't seen since 1993 either. My husband joined me in Matala and we came together to Galangue.

This woman was interviewed in the MSF feeding centre where three of her children were being treated for severe malnutrition. They had been brought to Caala from Chipindo by MSF. Chipindo was one of the towns where the FAA grouped civilians brought out of the bush during the scorched earth campaign. Like Bunjei the town fast ran out of food, and then remained inaccessible to humanitarian aid until the end of the war. The local authorities recorded 3,975 civilian deaths in Chipindo between September 2001 and April 2002, out of a total population of around 14,000.

I was very hungry. We only had sweet potatoes to eat; we used them to make flour. There was no soap, there were no clothes. People died all swollen up with oedema. Little cuts grew and people died. There were many deaths; 30 each day, sometimes 50, children and also adults. I arrived in Chipindo on January 1, 2002. I was brought there by the FAA with my husband and six children. One of my children died in Chipindo, in March because of oedema, hunger and diarrhoea. Before going to Chipindo we'd been in the forest, we were taken there by UNITA. I come from Chiconguele. Everything was fine there; we had food, livestock, cattle, and land to farm. UNITA bothered us a bit, they used to steal maize and if we didn't let them they would kill us. But I never actually saw anyone killed by UNITA, I just heard about it. UNITA attacks started in 1995. They happened almost every week, three or four times a month. In the beginning they took the cattle, then the maize, then the clothes, then the cooking things. They didn't capture people because, in any case, we were already under their control. I stayed there because I was afraid, and because we had food there. Afterwards the FAA arrived in December 2001 and surrounded us but they didn't kill anyone. They explained that we had to follow them to Chipindo or Matala. We were very happy to follow them. We walked for three days to reach Chipindo. They even gave us food on the way. We set off with nothing in a group of about 30 people. They burnt our houses. I was with my husband and my four children. I reached Chipindo on January 1. When we arrived, the people who had relatives had to go and stay with them in Lubango, Matala and other places. The soldiers took them. The rest stayed behind with the *sobas* and my husband built a hut for our family.

We'd been there three weeks when the diseases started appearing. When we arrived there were a lot of people there and, at the end of January, everyone started dying from disease. Since there was nothing to eat we made flour out of sweet potatoes which made the children swell up and get sick. The old people also got sick. We used to go and look for sweet potatoes in our areas of origin accompanied by FAA soldiers. We would walk for three days to get there, stay for three days, and then walk three more days to get back to Chipindo. Afterwards we stayed in Chipindo for two days before setting off again. Our whole group used to go – 30 people. I would go one time and my husband would go the next time. We didn't take the children so that we would be able to carry more sweet potatoes on the way back. The soldiers also took sweet potatoes for themselves. Whatever we could carry, we could keep for ourselves, except for one plateful which we had to give to them to thank them for accompanying us. My son died after one month there, in February, from an illness. He was three years old. Now I am here [in the feeding centre] with three children of seven, five and three years old. I left two boys aged 10 and eight in Chipindo. The youngest one has been sick since the end of March, and the other two as well. It was MSF who brought me here from Chipindo. We are well treated here. When the little ones are better I will go back to Chipindo and, from there, I will try to go to Matala because I've just learnt that my brother is there. I don't want to go back to Chiconguela.

♀
Caala
May 2002

This woman had also been brought to Caala from Chipindo with her two children, who were receiving treatment for severe malnutrition in the MSF feeding centre. She was originally from the village of Chitata.

In the forest we were fine but we weren't calm, there was food there but the problems started in Chipindo. In Chipindo we slept well, nobody bothered us, but we had nothing to eat. Chitata is a big village, we used to farm there and we even had four cows, other people had cows as well. I had four children, my husband worked in the administration of Chipindo. There are no local people left in Chipindo, only displaced people. There's an FAA commander who brings all of the people out of the forest to Chipindo. I came on my own with my husband and children because of the war, nobody brought us. In Chitata UNITA attacked constantly, the soldiers killed the people who stayed behind. One day, while we were running away I saw members of my family being murdered. We managed to run away. UNITA came all the time, sometimes in the morning, sometimes at night; they killed everyone who could not manage to escape. They stole the animals, then the food, then the clothes, and then the cooking utensils...everything. The boys were killed because UNITA said they belonged to the MPLA, and the girls too because they said they were members of JOTA [the MPLA youth movement], so they killed them too. As for the small children and the old people, they took them away with them.

I had four children – two died. One in the forest near Chitata in June 2001, he was 15 and he fell sick and died a short while later. The other died in Chipindo in August 2001, she was three and she died of a sickness with her stomach all swollen up. We set off for Chipindo in June 2001, after the death of the first child. In June 2000, the government troops attacked our village and stole all of our cattle. At that time UNITA accused my husband of giving information to the MPLA so that they would come and take the cattle and they wanted to kill him. He found out about that and ran away to Chipindo. I was made a prisoner in June 2000 and was always under guard. I was raped many times, I was forced to lie down with the soldiers, otherwise they would have killed me. I was forced to do anything they wanted. I went to fetch maize, I did all sorts of jobs for the commanders, I was a prisoner and my punishment was to do everything. The same thing happened to all the women whose husbands had run away. There were 30 of us suffering the same fate. We ate the leaves that we cooked for them. It was at that time that my first child died. When I went to fetch the maize the soldiers would hold the children hostage so that I couldn't run away but they never mistreated them. I didn't leave at the same time as my husband because at that time my son was already sick, he couldn't walk. And later on, in June 2001, there was a lot of confusion because the FAA attacked and UNITA wanted to run away to another place. In the middle of all of that upset I manage to escape with my three children. I walked, just with them, until we got to Chipindo, where I found my husband who had already arranged a job in the administration [he was responsible for registering deaths]. The journey to Chipindo was very hard. My three-year-old daughter started to get sick and she died two weeks later. At that time lots of people hadn't started dying yet because there was still maize. But later on, from September, there was no more maize, only sweet potatoes. I was alright because my husband had a job, although he was never paid. It was like that until last Monday, when the doctors brought me here with my 10-year-old daughter and my eight-year-old son. When my children are better I will go back to Chipindo and we will get on with our lives.

⚲

Bunjei
May 2002

This man had arrived with his family from Chipindo the day before the interview, having learnt that he could receive help from MSF in Bunjei. Having been examined in Bunjei, his severely malnourished son had been referred by MSF to the therapeutic feeding centre in Caala.

I am originally from the Chipindo area. I was born during the colonial times but I'm not sure exactly how old I am, about 50. I used to be a merchant in Lubango and I stayed there for many years. I had a house there that I built, with one bedroom and a living room. In 1991, when there was peace, the government said that all the people; who had come from Chipindo had to go back there because peace had arrived. I sold my house. In Chipindo there are a lot of people, there is a sort of hospital but there are no medicines. In January, more than 50 people were dying there each day. In the whole village all you could hear was

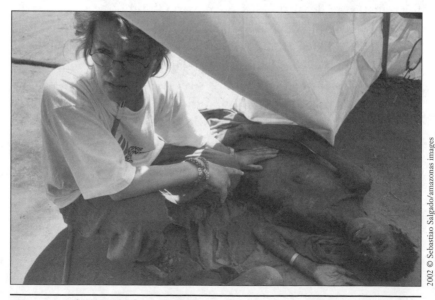

MSF nurse taking care of a severely malnourished woman in Bunjei. Bunjei 2002.

2002 © Sebastiao Salgado/amazonas images

people crying, and it's a big village. In Chipindo there is starvation; in January, February, March, the people had nothing to eat for days at a time. Sometimes they managed to leave the village to go and collect some sweet potatoes, but they don't nourish a person, so the people got anaemia and died. The people don't leave Chipindo, even if they know that MSF have been working in [nearby] Bunjei for quite some time because they don't have the strength. They don't have the strength to carry the sick people, and so they die. We arrived in Chipindo in August [2001], from the village of Sachagombé, two hours walk from Chipindo. Sachagombé is in the bush. I arrived there in 1997, and since then I never stopped running from the village, returning, running again and returning again, depending on rumours about FAA attacks and UNITA orders. Then we were captured by the government during an attack in which many, many people died. The government soldiers took us to Chipindo. In the last two years, I have lost seven children because of the war. They all died of anaemia, of hunger because there was nothing to eat in Chipindo. The oldest was 14 when he died, he didn't even have time to get married. All the children died. There was no more blood to give them a chance to live – even if you did [give them a blood transfusion], our blood wouldn't have helped them to live, nor could traditional medicine. It was only modern medicine which could perhaps have saved them. That's why when I saw that I wouldn't be able to get any medicines in Chipindo, I ran like a crazy man to bring my sick child here – to save my son. Between January 2 of this year and today [May 4, 2002], four of my children have died of starvation. They were all under 14 years old. Last year three children died. My daughter died in April, and two others died in August, the month when we arrived in Chipindo. In Chipindo I had a field which I tended, but I never saw the harvest. When the time came to harvest the crops the government soldiers came and took everything. They didn't give us anything. They were fields of maize. In Chipindo I was living in a grass hut. Today I have two children who are still alive, they are eight and nine. I am here with my wife and one of my two children who is very sick. What will I do now? Look after the health of my family, take my wife and my sick child to Caala [where he had been referred to the MSF feeding centre] and then go back to Chipindo to my other child.

Chipindo
August 2002

In August 2001, the enemy [FAA] surprised us at around three in the morning, in Canjivale Velho, close to Setor base. My wife was then taken by the FAA and I hid, together with other families in the river beds, close to the mountains. From where I hid, I could see when she was taken. My children were living with my father, in the Galangue area because where we were the fighting was constant and Galangue was calmer. We use to hide our cattle there too.

Four women and one man from my neighbourhood were caught and taken to Cachanguite, in Matala. No one died during that night but a child died the following morning. When the soldiers came and gathered the people, there was one child who cried a lot. The baby was five months old. So, they hit the mother with a wooden stick, in the head and then they did the same thing with the child. I know that because in the morning, after they'd left, I went back to the village and this woman was there with her child. We took the boy to the hospital close to Zona base. There was no wound and no blood but the boy died soon after. When he has hit the night before his head must have been broken. I buried the child myself and the mother and her husband stayed with us. Later on they went to Jamba. The soldiers found us because they were taken to where we were by three of the women they'd captured the day before. These women were from our neighbourhood and they knew where the cattle were. We had just fetched some cows from the hiding place in Galangue. They were an enormous group of soldiers, maybe around 150 men. And they came with the intention to loot the area because we were really close to a UNITA base. At that time we had cattle and a lot of food – maize, beans, cassava, sweet potato, sugar cane, soya beans and bananas.

Starting in 1999 we were often attacked by the FAA but their attacks became more frequent in 2001. The soldiers would come from Matala, Dongo and Jamba. They would take people, kill people and take our belongings. They took our clothes, our furniture and they'd burn our homes; we had nothing left. Later on they started coming from Chipindo also. In our area we hardly had any peace because the area was very UNITA; they [FAA] were always after us to see if we were soldiers. Starting in 1999 we'd stay more or less one month in any one place. Before then we had already been moving a lot but we'd spend more time in each place with no need to hide in the bush. We remained in the same area the whole time, around Setor base, in the municipality of Chipindo. The base was very big and it would move around also. Even the cattle were taken along.

In October [2001], my father came to Canjivale with my children and other relatives because the FAA from Bunjei started to come down to attack them. Most people from my father's neighbourhood were taken. We remained in Canjivale until February, then we got tired and decided to come to Chipindo. We got here on February 8, [2002]. We came to Chipindo in a small group, with my parents, my mother-in-law, my sons, a brother, my grandfather, three women and 15 children. We came during the day. In fact, the FAA came to attack and, as UNITA were busy with them, we took the opportunity to flee. We walked for two days and no one died on the way. We chose Chipindo because it was closer, and because there were UNITA troops on the way to Dongo and Matala. We knew there was hunger in Chipindo but where we were the war was too much. It was better to go to Chipindo and put up with the hunger there. We knew there was hunger because, as we still had food, people who'd been caught by the FAA and taken to Chipindo were coming back to stay and they were telling us that there was hunger in Chipindo. Last time I harvested corn was in September 2001. After that, we no longer had time to cultivate but we had a lot of food still. Then, UNITA started taking our food and the FAA was destroying our food. If they found it they'd burn it so that we wouldn't have enough but the area was very productive and we kept cultivating small parcels of land for family consumption during our displacements.

When the FAA captured Chipindo, life became very difficult. They were attacking a lot, from Nboe up to Gangueve and Camassissa, where they'd join up with the troops coming from Bunjei. In the area of Cuanjivale, the troops from Matala and Dongo would join the troops from Chipindo. The territory was kind of divided by the troops from different areas and the people who were in between suffered a lot, they lived badly. When we arrived in Chipindo there were not many people from our neighbourhood because most of them had been taken to Matala, Jamba and Dongo. A lot of families were separated because of that. We were shown a place to build our houses and Commander Cacolo gave us two kilograms of flour per family. Two weeks later he gave us three kilograms per family plus blankets and coats because we had nothing when we came. The mortality situation in Chipindo was bad and there were a lot of diseases because we had only sweet potato to make into flour. There was nothing else. If you had money you could buy maize from the FAA. They had food and part of it was given to the people. Then in March we started going to fetch goods in the fields we had left behind. Those fields were in the hands of UNITA but, as we came with the FAA, UNITA would run away. Until May we continued doing that, but then the food ran out completely. We had no permission to leave Chipindo on our own. The FAA would not give anyone permission to leave. Many people fled back to UNITA areas anyway and were well received by UNITA. But if the FAA found you on the way you would not remain alive. The first ones to get to Chipindo were the ones that were caught by the FAA. The ones who came later came on their own because the war intensified and they couldn't go two weeks without being attacked.

The FAA arrived in Kahuiki some time in the middle of 2000. I know that because I was there for Easter. The FAA told the people to come with them to Luquembo. Most people went, though some stayed behind. My family left because UNITA was coming and was going to take the people of the village into the bush with them. It was right then that the FAA arrived. UNITA did take some people, and followed all of us when we left with the FAA. That same day we started towards Luquembo, the FAA indicated an area and told us to sleep. The FAA took a position in front of us. Then UNITA attacked from the rear and we all fled. The FAA fled too. UNITA took me and 19 other young men, along with five women. They bound our arms behind our backs and took us away. When we got to a bridge over a rushing river, they shot us, and pushed us in the water, our arms still tied, though not the girls, who they took with them. I was shot in the backside…somehow I managed to get out of the river. I was the only survivor. UNITA wasn't waiting for me because they thought we were all dead. I broke my ropes and walked alone to Luquembo (on both arms the boy had scars from where he was bound just above the elbow). Although I was shot, I walked to Loquembo on my own. There, at the hospital, they could not cure me. They gave me some salve but they didn't even have any bandages. They didn't have any supplies. After some time, a military helicopter brought me to the Malange Provincial Hospital. They also brought my mother and brothers and sisters, but my father could not come because his name was not on the list. I haven't seen him since. From Malange, the family moved to Cangandala because we didn't know anybody in Malange. Here, my aunt had already arrived, she had run away earlier. My problem is that I don't have any clothing and that there is not enough food.

**Matala
February 2001**

I came here with my mother and my younger brother and sisters. My father was killed by UNITA in 1997. They came to the house and they were looking for me. I would always run away to the bush when they came. My father was in the house and they asked him, "Why does your son not want to be a solider with us? We think that you are on the side of the MPLA" – so they took him and killed him with a machete. One day UNITA found me in the fields looking after the cows. I was with my two little brothers. They took me and beat me with a stick in the side here. Blood was coming out of my mouth and nose. They said, "We cannot take him now he is like this, we will leave him here to die." It was not too far from my house and when they were beating me, I cried out and my mother recognised my voice. When they left, my mother came and took me home. After this we all fled with a group of people. We were very scared because we were walking at night and we didn't know if we would meet the FAA or UNITA. We were afraid to meet them both because if UNITA caught us leaving they would kill us and if the FAA found us they would kill us because we were UNITA's people.

The FAA never came to the village to ask for food, but they passed through on the way to Chipindo. In June last year [2000] the FAA came and took all of our cows. Some people left with the FAA but UNITA always told us "soon there will be peace," so we never left because we did not want to leave our fields and our cows. Most people would flee to the bush when the FAA came. We did not run away when UNITA came because we were UNITA's people. It's like if the FAA comes here [a government controlled town], we don't have to run but if UNITA comes they will kill us because now we are on the side of the MPLA. In 1999, the FAA came and took a lot of people from our village. They took them far away but then they decided that there were too many, so they killed some of the people. I was not there, but my friend was and he escaped and came back to the village. He saw the FAA killing the people. I am 18 years old and I have never been to school. I am happy to be here on the government side. I will never go back there.

11-year-old boy
Malange
January 2001

UNITA? UNITA are like grasshoppers…they kill everything. My mother was killed by the FAA. She went to the market to sell some tomatoes; some FAA soldiers started to hassle her, asking for some of the tomatoes. Then the military police came and all of a sudden there was a confusion; the FAA and the military police started shooting at each other. My mother was shot. My father took her to the hospital but she died…. It made me very angry with the FAA.

"Without peace you cannot be happy. Now we can think about the future, dream about the future. During the war we could only dream about more war."

– Man, Cuimba. March 2003.

And Now Peace...

As time passes, peace is becoming a tangible entity for the people of Angola. Millions of the displaced have been making their way back to homes that many haven't seen in years. IDP camps have been closing as their inhabitants scatter throughout Angola. Hundreds of thousands of refugees in neighbouring countries also have been returning home. Villages, emptied of people, burnt to the ground and enveloped by the bush, are coming back to life. The bush is being cleared, new houses are emerging amongst the ruins of the old, and new crops are being planted. Angola's roads, until recently the domain only of the desperate, are now are creaking under the weight of the traffic using them. Goods are flowing and prices are falling. Perhaps most poignantly, thousands of families have been reunited with loved ones whom they had long assumed to be dead. The impenetrable barrier which had been constructed between the two sides has crumbled, generations taken to the bush by UNITA have returned to their families in the cities. Hope has been reborn, and the impossible is beginning to seem possible.

We should rejoice in Angola's peace, but we should not forget that Angola is a country which needs to be rebuilt – physically and socially. More importantly, we must remember the serious problems that exist now. Humanitarian organizations have spent years delivering food and healthcare to people condensed in government-held areas and camps. Many have returned home, spreading themselves over the breadth of Angola, far from available healthcare or clean water, beyond the reach of food distributions for those still in need. Landmines still litter the countryside, rendering even simple tasks such as planting a seed, dangerous. For instance, a landmine was found on the "cleared" road to be used for the repatriation of tens of thousands of refugees living in Zambia.

The narratives in this section were taken within two years after the end of the fighting. They vividly demonstrate that, in the minds of those who have survived the conflict, peace is, as yet, just a moment in a lifetime of war. When asked to speak about what peace means for them, our interviewees still spoke mainly about war. But at least, as these testimonies show, Angolans are already beginning to reflect on the war through the softening lens of peace.

♂

M'banza Congo
March 2003

This man was interviewed as he was about to be flown back to his home province after being given permission to leave the UNITA demobilisation camp where he'd been living since the cease-fire.

I'm from the Province of Uige, from the municipality of Maquela de Zombo. The last time I was there was four years ago. I'm 47 years old. I left Maquela because of the war. I was a commander in UNITA. I've been in UNITA since 1988. Did I join UNITA out of political conviction? Well, the war was a situation that forced all of us, all of the nation, you know. It was a question of obligation.... It happened when I wasn't there. I was away, and when I came back home I found that the *sobas* had already given my name, they'd put my name on the list for UNITA and there was no way to get out of it.[57] I was already 32 years old then. Before I entered UNITA I was a tailor. I had a family; I had three children already – who today are in Luanda. I had to leave them behind and I've never had any contact with them ever again, it just wasn't possi-

---

[57] In areas under their control UNITA frequently instructed the *sobas* to hand over a certain number of men and boys from their village to be trained as soldiers.

2004 © Kadir van Lohuizen

Psychiatric hospital in Malange. Malange 2004

ble. My first daughter now is 22, my second, a son, is 19, and the third is 17. I had those children in the time of Agostinho Neto.[58] My first wife also stayed behind; now I have another wife. Throughout the war I was always in our province of Uige. It was only towards the end of the war that I came here, to Zaire province. Did I like military life? At that time, whether you liked it or not, you had to like it because you had to take part in it. If you tried to get away from it, you were prevented. You did the job, made it to the end, and now it's over…it's over. We were waiting for there to be a good peace, good justice, a situation where the people all realised there was no more point having war, where the people learnt to value each other, to live with each other and share their riches. And now that we have that, it is a source of satisfaction for all of us and we embrace it. My life was a bit affected by the war because during wartime a person can't think right, because the country is not calm. War destroys. It does not organise, it disorganises. And it also disorganises people's thoughts; people can't complete their thoughts in a war because they're not living in a calm situation. My life still hasn't changed much since peace because I still don't have the means to build a house like this house, for example. My life is still confined to ideas. With my age, I am thinking a lot about whether I am going to be able to work properly again, whether I will manage to build a decent house. But at least now, thanks to peace, each one of us can use our efforts to work, and to develop, to achieve our objectives. In a war a person cannot develop, you can't develop anything, you can just survive. I think this peace process is going well. If it wasn't going well things would have started to happen – in the past, in the other processes for example, a person [from UNITA] could be walking down the street and he'd be assaulted, beaten up. That's what happened. Or you could be at home, in bed, and the police would come and beat on your door and take you away. But this time that's not happening, so we believe that this process is serious. This is the peace that all Angolans have been waiting for. I want to try and get a job now, to try to build up a life again. And I'd like to go to Luanda to find my children there. I haven't seen them for such a long time, I miss them. There has to be national reconcil-

---

[58] Angola's first president, in power from 1975 until 1979.

iation now because this war was not born in Angola, it was born in the outside world, for its own reasons. This war started a very long time ago, before we were even born. So when someone understands that the war started in the time of his grandparents, and that it has finally finished, there has to be understanding, reconciliation. This peace has come to stay, it has come to stay. Inside of us, it is here to stay.

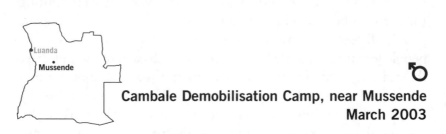

Cambale Demobilisation Camp, near Mussende
March 2003

I am 35 years old. I'm from Catabola, in Bié Province. I left Catabola in 1976 because of the war. When the Cubans invaded Huambo we had no real idea about who they were or what they would do, so we had to retreat into the bush. I was seven years old then. I went with my parents. My strongest memories from that period were of the suffering we lived through until we reached Jamba. That lasted for years. After we got to Jamba I grew up and studied there, until I reached the age for joining the [UNITA] army. I fought in the army for 10 years, defending our stronghold. I fought in Cuito Cuanavale, Yonde, Moxico, etc.. Combat is hard; it makes human lives disappear very easily. The worst thing about the war for me was that I burnt up the whole of my youth in fighting when I should have been sitting behind a desk, studying at university. But it was worth it because it wasn't in vain. If we hadn't fought, we would have been killed. If I could have gone to university I would have studied electrical engineering. Even now that's a dream that I still have. If I could study now, I would do electrical engineering. My life has changed substantially thanks to peace. Where before I had to use up all of my energy and imagination thinking about military strategy, about managing men and weapons and war material, now I don't have to – I can just think about the reconstruction of the country, about the development of my children, and make projects for the future. That is already a very big change, very big. I have 10 children – all of them are still alive. I just received word from Bailundo that two of my children that I left there are in good health.

The memories of the war are still very fresh. But that's an old hatchet that we have to bury, and we have to think instead about the evolution of peace. Every day that passes I feel a bit better than the one before because we can see that this peace has really come to stay. This is not another fictitious peace. In the last peace process anyone from UNITA who presented themselves was killed by the government. There was a lot of fear and mistrust. This time too, we were very afraid that the same thing would happen, but we can see that the FAA have made a big effort and nothing bad has happened, no one has been killed. There are still some bad memories though. For example, yesterday a helicopter passed by here and all of the children started running away, thinking that the war had come back. But since we're living in a new context now, we're forgetting these things, little by little. If anyone wants to start another war in this Angola, he will have to fight against his own children because no one else will accept another war – never again. That would be a horrible nightmare. It's part of our black, African tradition that after the death of our loved ones we have to bury them properly. And now, with the end of the war, we are able to do that at last. For example in this camp, two days ago, we had a ceremony to mark the end of the mourning period for one of our commanders who died in combat one year ago. The whole family gathered together and there was a ritual, with people dancing and drumming, and in that way the family felt satisfied, they felt relieved. That has been happening a lot since peace.

ᄒ
Village near Mussende
March 2003

I was born in 1937. I am 66 years old. I was born here, just on the other side of that stream there. The village always used to be over there, on that side of the stream. But in 1992, when we came back here for the first time, I moved it from there to here because here we're closer to the fields and to the water.[59] We spent the war here, with UNITA, suffering. At any time of day or night you had to walk, whenever they told you. We suffered. During the government's last offensive we were in the bush. We heard that the FAA had taken Andulo, then they took Mussende, and then we went to hand ourselves over to the FAA in Mussende, in 2001. But then in Mussende there was hunger, there was no food, so we asked the commander for a document, for permission to return to our fields to get some food. But on the way we ran into UNITA, they caught us and took us back into the bush. We couldn't run away because they'd captured the whole family, and if one person escaped, they would kill all of the others. So we had to stay with them until we heard that Savimbi had died. Then the peace came and we left there and came back here, to the village. That's when I built this house. Then the other people who had left here heard that I had come back, that I was living in the village again, rebuilding, and so the population also started coming back. Now there are 26 houses here but the majority of the people still haven't come because they don't have the money to pay for the transport, for the car and for the canoe. There used to be 450 people in this village, but most of them are still living on the other side of the River Cuanza [where they sought refuge in IDP camps during the war]. They had planned to return in January, but they didn't come. Now they're talking about May. And there are others who went as far as Luanda but they have sent us a letter saying that they want

---

[59] This man was the *soba* of his village.

to come back too, saying that they ran away because of the war, but now that the war is over they want to come back. They're just waiting to find the money for the journey.

When I came back here there was no one here, not a single house, not a single field, it was just bush. The houses had all been burnt. There were just a couple of walls left here and there. All the houses that you see here are new, we built them. The people had all left, some to Mussende town, some to Cangandala, some to Luanda. By the end it was just me and my family who were still in the bush. UNITA arrived here in 1974; from then on it has just been war here. In 1983, we left and went to live on the government side, over there on the other side of the River Cuanza. We were running away from the war. We stayed there for 17 years. They gave us a bit of land there, for me and my people, and we rebuilt our village there. We came back in 1992, when there was that mini-peace. The government said that the war was over, so the people decided to go back home. We got back here and then the war fell on our heads all over again. And by then UNITA was occupying everywhere that we could have escaped to, so we couldn't escape, we just had to stay here with them. The worst thing in the war was walking day and night. We, the 450 people

People have started farming again. Malange 2004

here, were obliged to produce 1,500 kilograms of cassava flour every week and transport it to the front lines on our heads. If you didn't do it, you were killed. Now with peace I'm much, much better. We are sleeping better, there's no more fear, no more thoughts of the war; all of our thoughts now are about working, to find something to eat and something to wear, and maybe a bicycle. There are so many people who are alone now. They don't have any family left – UNITA killed them all. We don't want any more war. The people are so tired. We spent all the time running; either you ran, or UNITA caught you and took you to the bush, and then so many people died. They died in the fighting or they died because they were executed. We've had enough dying. What we've lost is lost. We can't force anyone to compensate us for what we've lost. Maybe my bicycle was lost, or maybe my mattress, but they're gone. What we want is life, to be able to work again, to be able to buy another bicycle or another mattress. What is gone is gone. Now the children are going to school. The mothers and the fathers, they can go to the field or to the market, they can go about their work with no fear, thinking, "Ah, my child is in school, safe." And when they finish working they can go and find their child. Who studied during the war? No one.

♀

Village near Mussende
March 2003

I am 22 years old. I was born near here, but in 1983 we left to go and live in Malange Province, and we stayed there for 18 years. During the peace of 1992 we left Malange and came back to near here, where we rebuilt our village but then the war started up again and UNITA came. We stayed with them for a while but then it got too bad and we left again, and went back to Malange, to Cangandala, where we lived in an IDP camp. It wasn't too bad; we got food from the UN and other humanitarian organisations. It wasn't a question of liking it or not liking it, we just had to accept it. We went because of the war, not because we wanted to. The war has cost me a lot. There have been times when I have lived well, owned a lot of things, but now all of that has disappeared, the war took all of it. Now, to get a bit of soap or some salt I have to run around, fetching maize from here carrying it into town to the market and seeing if I can exchange it for something else. The worst thing in the war was that we ate badly, we were weak and had no energy, but still we were forced to carry very heavy loads over long distances for UNITA. Loads like this (indicates something as high as her shoulder) it was awful...suffering.... I can't tell you.

With peace, we're not suffering like we used to suffer before. We're not carrying loads or weapons for UNITA. We can stay in one place. I came back here to the village in June. I felt there was peace and so I came back. We weren't forced by anyone to come; it was the choice of every person or every family. I was very happy to return. But when we got here, the village was completely destroyed. When we first arrived we sheltered behind that wall (points at a wall which is all that is left of an old house). We didn't have anything to eat. There was nothing left in our fields here, but it's getting better now because we are working in our fields. Clothes are a bigger problem. Where are we going to get money to buy them (laughs)? It's the same problem with soap and salt. But still, no one intimidates us here now, and we have managed to rebuild our houses. Hopefully in the next few years things will get better. I don't know if this peace is different from the last ones. The ones who know that are the bosses, the leaders; they're the ones who know if the peace will last.

♀
Cuimba
March 2003

I'm from Cuimba but I came back here recently because, as is usual here, when there's war here you can't stay here – you have to do everything possible to escape. I was in the refugee camp in Kilueka[60] and I came back at the end of 2001. I'm 42 years old now – that child that's crying over there (points to a boy who looks about three), he's my grandson. The last time we left here was in 1998. It was a Tuesday. I'd recently had a baby who wasn't even three months old yet. I saw all the people running and I said, "Eh? What's going on?" and they said, "Quick lady, where's your husband? Get ready because the enemy's already close to Cuimba." And outside all the people were running by with their possessions on their heads. I didn't have time to prepare anything. I just picked up the things for the baby and waited for my husband to come. He was in the school teaching. He scolded me and said "Ay ay ay – what are you still doing here? Everyone else is already miles away from Cuimba and you're still here?" So he ran to the market to fetch one of our children who was there, and he told me to take the children and head for the border with Congo. He said he had to stay behind because he worked for the government. I went with eight children, including small children, one was three another was five. There was no means of transport and we were trembling and wondering if we'd ever make it to the border. So we went on foot, but the little children couldn't walk well. We went 20 kilometres from Cuimba in the first day. The children were crying; I didn't know what to do. We spent the night there. It was near the big river so there were many mosquitoes; we hardly slept at all. The next day we got to Buela, on the border, but the Angolan border officials told me that I was not allowed to pass because I was also a teacher. They said the government had not given permission for its employees to cross the border. Everyone was passing, and it was just me who was stuck there with the children. I stayed there four days. Then, after four days, my husband came. He said the situation in Cuimba was getting too dangerous, he couldn't stay behind; he had to run away too. He thought we must already be in Congo. When he found us still in Buela he was very cross. He told me I was a wicked woman, but then I explained what happened, so he went to the border to talk to those men. So then

---

[60] In the Democratic Republic of Congo, formerly Zaire.

they let us across and my husband accompanied us as far as a town on the other side. All that distance on foot, with the children crying and the hot sun above us. When we arrived there, there was no refugee camp. They only built the camp later on. First of all we went to somewhere called Posto 18 but we only stayed there for two weeks because I quickly saw that every day, every day, the children were dying. They were dying of hunger or illness; there wasn't food or medicine. There were many cemeteries there. So we left there and went to Lucala. My husband's nephew lives there, so we stayed with him for a while. But then I got to a point where I was thinking: "Ah, but I am an adult, the mother of a family. I'm used to managing my own household, and here I'm living in another woman's house. We're trying to live here together, I'm completely dependent on them, and that's just a headache for everyone. It's better if I find a little house for myself." So we moved out of that house for a short while. But things were not good.

Then some of the children went to buy something a way away, and when they came back they said: "Mother, we're suffering here for nothing. There's a refugee camp not far from here where the people are living much better than we are. They have hospitals and food and everything." So we set off for the camp. We moved

Food distribution in Malange. Malange 2004

2004 © Kadir van Lohuizen

there in 1999 and stayed there until we came back here. I thought that once we got there we would receive rice, sardines, oil, all of those good things but in fact all we got was some dried beans and some awful oil. They sent good oil, soya oil, but a crooked man working in that camp took it and sold it and bought old palm oil instead. With that oil, if you were here, and someone was cooking with it right over there (points to a house about 20 metres away), it would make you cough. It gave us all a cough and diarrhoea.

We stayed there until late in 2001. We came back here even before war had ended because life there was too difficult. My husband had come back here earlier. For years he didn't know where we were. He made a big effort, a big journey; he went to Luanda, from there to Cabinda, and from there by boat to Congo. He went to his nephew's house, and there he learnt that we were in the refugee camp. He came to see us there and found us living in horrible conditions. He'd planned just to come for a quick visit but he ended up staying for a year to try and help us there. He started trading, buying fish there, carrying it on his head to somewhere else, selling it there, then buying something else and bringing it back again. Always like that. But it was too tiring so he decided to come home. He came back to M'banza Congo and was appointed vice-administrator for Cuimba. That was in 2001. I was still in Congo with the children but they were always sick. One came out of the hospital, then another got sick and went in. And I couldn't bear it, I thought, "If I stay here much longer I will lose my children here. It's better to go." So at first I left the children there and I came on my own. At that time UNITA was massacring people here. I found a boy with a bicycle and he transported me on the back of his bicycle, from the camp to the border, and from the border to here. I found my husband here and said: "I can't bear life as a refugee any longer. If we stay there, and you stay here, one of these days you're going to be receiving bad news about us. You'd better make plans to go and fetch the children." So we went and got the children. We had to wait for a week before we could set off because UNITA was attacking people on the road. In the three years we'd been away, the children hadn't managed to learn a thing in school. They kept failing their exams and repeating the same class because they didn't understand when the teacher spoke French.

The first war that came here was in 1987. When that happened we fled to Kinshasa and stayed there until 1991. In 1991, everyone was saying "Peace, peace, peace" so we came home. We hadn't even been here a year when the war started up again. We'd planned to move to Luanda but we couldn't because of the problem of the elections. We decided that we had to vote here, we couldn't vote in Luanda. But by the time the elections were over it was too late – the war had started again. UNITA took Cuimba and we were here as their prisoners, which was awful, you have to work for them for nothing, grow food, make cooking oil, cut trees. How can you feed your family when you're doing that? All the men ran away and the women were left doing men's work for UNITA. The men couldn't stay; UNITA didn't like to see the men here. If they caught a man, even if he's just a simple worker, a teacher, UNITA would say he was into politics, working for the MPLA. All the men were scared so they ran and hid in the bush. We women stayed here on our own until 1998 when the government came. Then we started working normally again and receiving our salaries. When the third war started here, this one from 1998, we didn't hang about here. That's what made us go to Congo. The first war was bad because it was the first time I'd heard that crashing of the weapons. The second war was about the same. This third one was the worst. War is always war. War always creates difficulties. When war comes you go straight outside, call your children, and off you go, with nothing to eat and nothing to wear and nowhere to sleep. Since this peace came we are giving thanks to God because it's God who gave us peace. This is not the peace of some man or other, it's from God. We still have a lot of problems here – problems of electricity, of water. For our lives to really change all these broken bridges around here need to be fixed, the houses need to be repaired, the roads, the schools, the hospitals. Have you seen the refugees coming back from Congo now? They're all coming on foot with tiny children and they're suffering, lots of them. Why? Because there are no bridges on the roads to here, they were all destroyed in the war and now the trucks can't get here. And so they walk. They come with no money, nothing. How are they going to live?

I saw one lady pass here recently with four children under the age of seven. Who's going to carry them? The woman had all their things on her head and a baby on her back. The children all had swollen feet, they could hardly stand up. They'd already walked four days and they weren't home yet – it's too much suffering. But they come home because life is too hard in Congo. At least here they're free. The land here is theirs, it's good, and if they use it no one abuses them. In Congo all the land belonged to the people there. You had to work on their land for them, grow their crops and when it came time to harvest they'd take all the best produce for themselves and just leave you a small part, and there was nothing you could say. That's why people are coming back. Leaving all their belongings behind and coming home to their land. But the people here suffer. We have no doctors. From here to the nearest hospital it's 69 kilometres. That's a long way. Whenever they try to evacuate a sick person from here to the hospital, they get 30 kilometres from here and drop dead. But life is different since the peace and we're praying hard because we don't want more war. War holds up our lives. At my age, in a normal country, I could own many things. But here, every time the war flares up again, we lose everything.

We don't want more war, this peace has to last; we want peace forever. So the children can study. So the people become free, so they can work and eat and travel as they like. So that if someone in M'banza Congo wants to come to Cuimba, they can just come, knowing that no one will threaten them or abuse them on the way. My whole life has been in the time of the war. I don't like to think about that much – it gives me a pain in my heart. Here you can see a 10-year-old child; he already has a stomach problem. Why? From too much thinking and not enough food. In Congo I was there as a mother with eight children. I couldn't manage to feed them all. I was always getting stomach aches[61] from too much thinking. The children were all failing in school. I didn't know if my husband was alive or dead. I didn't know what to do. I'm a teacher but I can't teach anymore. The war has given me stomach aches. It makes you think, think, think too much. Ugh. And now I can't bear the noise of the children any more.

---

[61] Possibly stomach ulcers induced by stress.

2004 © Kadir van Lohuizen

School children in Malange. Malange 2004.

♀
Cuimba
March 2003

This woman had been living in a refugee camp in the Democratic Republic of Congo (DRC). She had returned from the DRC less than a week before the interview.

Before, the refugees in Congo used to receive a lot of help - food, medical care, lots of things. But now the situation has got much worse, they just get a little bit of food and in the health post there are almost no medicines. You go and they just give you one pill which you have to break in half and take half in the morning and half in the evening. The situation has become very difficult there. Before, when a woman gave birth in the refugee camps she received lots of support – clothes for the baby, soap, special food – but now, since there has been peace in Angola, all of that assistance has been stopped.

I was born here in Cuimba but I lived a long time in the Congo. We went to the Congo in 1998. For me it was my first time as a refugee. There was a lot of war here; we couldn't bear it so we had to go to Congo. The war was very strong, a lot of people died. I left with my husband and two children – one on my back and one in my arms. I am 25 years old now. We walked to the Congo, and when we got into the Congo we carried on, on foot. First of all we arrived in a town. We stayed there quite a long time until the cars came from the UNHCR[62] to fetch the people and evacuate them to a centre for refugees. In the beginning it was not a camp, it was just a big building in the town of Kimpese where we could stay because there was no camp for us. And then later on they made a camp for us in Kilueka. When we first got to that camp they treated us very well. When the children were sick they would evacuate them to a big hospital where they got good treatment. They gave us plenty of food, soya,

---

[62] United Nations High Commissioner for Refugees.

maize flour, but after they signed the peace accords here in Angola, they reduced the assistance there in Congo. They told us that the food we used to receive was going to other countries now. They said there were lots of other countries that were at war, and there wasn't enough food for us and them, so since Angola was already at peace they were cancelling our food. That happened in November 2002. They cancelled everything because they said the war in our country was over so we could already go home to our country and there was no point giving us much food in the Congo. So since there's been peace in Angola the refugees in the Congo have been a bit anxious because of those problems, so they are coming here on foot. Some have heard that the UNHCR is going to provide transport to move them, so some are waiting there for it. Those who have small children can't manage to walk with them, so they are putting up with the shortages in Congo and waiting for the transport. I came back on my own, with my baby. I left my other children behind because they can't walk. My husband came back here earlier. When I hear that the UNHCR is beginning to repatriate people I will go back to Congo to fetch my children. I left them there with my sister-in-law. I walked four days to get here, my feet are still sore. Still, I'm happy that there is peace, I'm happy that I can come back to my country. It's bad to live in a foreign country; I prefer to be in my own country. I've been away a long time. Now I have to start my life here from zero again because all of my things have been stolen. So I'm still working out how I am going to live here. It's still a bit strange for me to be here, it's hard to believe. I can't really believe that Angola's at peace. I do believe it, but at the same time…it's strange. All of the fields I left have been pillaged; my old house has fallen down because of the war. This house belongs to a relative. I'm going to do my best to build a new house, but the roof that I left behind on my old house has been stolen and it's hard to get roofing materials here.

ʕ̊

**Mussende
March 2003**

I'm from here, from Mussende, but I left in 1978. Since then I've only been here twice, each time for a couple of weeks. I live in Luanda. I was very affected by the war because if it weren't for the war I would have a lot more. But in fact all of my things were destroyed. I went to Luanda with nothing, like a displaced person, and I found it hard to build up any new life. And even living there, in the city, we felt the pain that the country was experiencing. The worst thing that happened during the war, for me, was the fact that I had five brothers who all disappeared and until today I have no idea what has happened to them. Maybe, if God helps us, one day one of them will reappear. I've looked for them in the demo-bilisation camps close to here, and they're not in any of them. Maybe they're in other camps, further away.

My life has changed a lot because of peace. It was difficult for us who were living in Luanda to come here to Mussende. But now we can come here without any trouble. I can already go 10 or 20 kilo-metres on foot in the bush around here without anything happen-ing to me. I hope that soon, with peace, Mussende will be beautiful again. I can really see the differences here. The people are in a much worse state, physically, than they used to be. Hopefully now they can get better. Our big challenge now is to get the roads open so that the businessmen can get goods into the town to help these people. At the moment they don't have clothes, some don't have enough food still, others are coming back from being displaced. I think that this time we have peace for good. The other times we didn't have much confidence but this time we do because this time all of the people are united. All UNITA people have come out of the bush for the first time. With pain, you feel it for the first couple of days, but then later you forget it. With work and changes you for-get the past and work towards making a new life.

ⵁ

**Mussende
March 2003**

I'm from here, from Mussende. My life was very affected by the war because it took my mother. She set off a landmine on August 5, 2001. And my oldest brother also trod on a mine, on November 6, 2000. That happened here in Mussende. Both of them stepped on mines on their way to the fields. I spent all of the war here. It was hard and very horrible. At my age I shouldn't have already lost my mother, my father, and other brothers who could have helped me in the future. After the last attack, which was on January 22, 2002, we had to run from here, abandon everything we had, and take refuge in Malange. We stayed there through February and March, and only came back here in April of last year. The worst things that happened during the war were hunger, nakedness, and death – people were dying because there were no medicines. They would get sick and die because the medicines couldn't get here because of the conditions imposed by the war. Those are the problems that affected the population of Mussende throughout the war. The absence of salt also, we used to eat food with no salt, no oil.

I was never a soldier; I didn't have to fight, but I am a nurse, and as a nurse I really had to struggle to try to help the young generation stay alive to be able to build the country. Fighting is not just with a weapon in your hand; someone who is struggling for the well-being of the people is also involved in a fight. My life has changed a bit because of peace because now we can sleep easily, even if all of our belongings are gone. But being able to sleep peacefully, being able to go fetch food from the fields without being constantly afraid of being surprised by people threatening to kill you, that means that life has changed. I have come back here to stay because this is the land of my birth. And already we are seeing developments here. For example, the hospital is already in much better condition than before – at least now we have some chairs and tables, some beds and some medicines. That's only been possible because of peace. Without peace MSF could never have come to Mussende. I don't feel the effects of the war in my life too badly. The war is over now. In my heart the pain doesn't go away, but I think we're already beginning to forget, to move forward. It's hard to forget everything that we've lost though, the pain doesn't end. But I don't dream about war any more, I think we used to dream about the war because we always felt threatened, we were always waiting for the next upset. But now that we don't feel threatened anymore we're dreaming about normal things. I think that peace has come to stay now, but everything depends on the spirits of the Angolans themselves. As long as men are prepared to let sense into their minds, then peace can come to stay. It's we who can make peace, so long as we agree to love our brothers. For me…the war…I don't really understand it. It took my whole family, and all of the killing was just between brothers. I can't really explain it. You have to ask the ones who were killing us. Today we're at peace and still no one can explain to us what was the reason for that war. I think the war stopped because those who were thinking badly of the people were convinced, with the passage of time, to stop. Because they realised that no one was

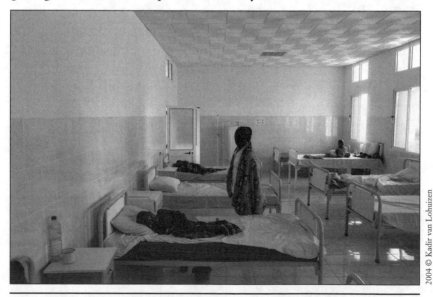

2004 © Kadir van Lohuizen

The new Tuberculosis ward in the Malange hospital. Malange 2004.

born to suffer forever. No one was born to suffer every day. Because people are born to develop, to study, to learn a trade, but we've all been regressing. People now have no trade, no education – everyone is illiterate because of the war. But now everyone is studying, that's really a visible change. Now everyone, from the children to the old men who are 60 years old, all of them are going to school.

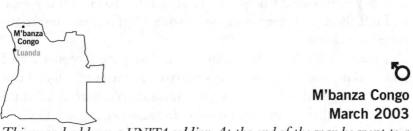

**M'banza Congo
March 2003**

This man had been a UNITA soldier. At the end of the war he went to a demobilisation camp in the Province of Uige before returning home to M'banza Congo for the first time in eight years.

I'm from M'banza Congo. I left here in 1995. In 1995, I went to [the UNITA controlled town of] Negage in Uige Province. I lived there for some time. I was with a boss, a Colonel from UNITA. From there we went up to Cabinda, where we stayed for a while. Then, when the last demobilisation process started in 1997, we left Cabinda and went back to Uige. We were in a demobilisation camp in Uige. After I was demobilised that time, we were allowed to go and mix with the people. So I went to Caculama, in Malange Province, where I was living as a civilian. I'm a driver so I was working as a minibus driver between Malange city and Milando. But when things changed again, when the war started again, it wasn't safe for me to go back to the city any more. I had the idea to go to Milando on foot, but on the way there I fell into a UNITA ambush and ended up back in their army. They allocated us to various companies, and we started fighting as guerrillas all over again. From there I was sent to the area of Cambundi Catembo, and while I was there I got this illness that I still have (pulls up his left trouser leg to show two suppurating wounds). Because of this I asked for a transfer to the area commanded by

General Apollo, in Baixo Cuango near Quimbele, back in Uige Province. I got permission so I went on foot – it's a very long way. We walked for two months and two weeks. Once I got there I was working for a Brigadier until the war ended, when we went up to Uamba [demobilisation camp]. Since my leg was still not better I was sent from there to Uige city for treatment, but the treatment didn't work, so the FAA prepared all of my demobilisation documents and I went to Luanda. In Luanda I stayed in the hospital, but they also couldn't help me. They wanted to cut off my foot, so I left there and came back here, where I'm undergoing traditional treatment.[63]

I joined UNITA in the beginning because the Colonel who I was working for is my uncle; he's married to my aunt. Since I was a driver, he decided to give me a job as his driver, here in M'banza Congo. So that made it look like I was working for UNITA. When the enemy, errr…I mean the government's troops arrived in M'banza Congo,[64] I thought that if I stayed behind, someone would betray me to the government troops, someone would say I was from UNITA, and then they would hunt me. So I decided to leave with the men from UNITA and from then on I got stuck with them, until now. Later on, when they lost their cars, then I became part of the guard for the Colonel. It's not that I chose military life, or that I liked it, it's just that I was obliged to go with them – it was the only thing to do. When you're with UNITA you have to seem always very cheerful. If you look sad, even just for a moment, then immediately they start to suspect you, they start to think, "Maybe this man is thinking about running away." And if they think that, then maybe they'll kill you or maybe they'll punish you. You can't keep to yourself in UNITA. The ones who carry out the punishment, they're in the same situation. They can't show sadness or regret because they're acting on orders from officers who are higher up than them. Military punishment in UNITA is either doing some gymnastics, or being put in prison, or being beaten with a stick. I never had to punish anyone and I never took part in an attack because I was always in the rearguard with the commanders, with the Colonel. It's the senior

---

[63] Administered by a *kimbanda* or herbalist, traditional treatments rely on the use of the roots, leaves and bark from certain plants.

[64] UNITA controlled the city of M'banza Congo from 1992 until 1995.

officers, from Lieutenant-Colonel and upwards, who control the frontline troops. They don't go to the front, they just send orders. In the areas where we were we didn't suffer too much from hunger. We were eating the food that had been left in the fields by the people who'd run away from their villages. I didn't like what UNITA was doing to the people there because my mother is also a farmer. So when we were there eating the food which belonged to the people, it was as if we were eating the food which my mother had worked to produce. And when those people go back to their villages, what will they have to eat? So no, I didn't like it. But at the same time we had no opportunity to grow food, so what were we meant to do?

I heard about the President's death [Savimbi] on February 22, 2002 – the same day that he died. We were still in the bush then, in Quimbele. That day we were attacked by the FAA and we all withdrew from our base. After we went back to the base my boss was going through the new radio messages which we'd received from the other UNITA commanders, and one of them said that Savimbi had been killed. As soon as my boss read that he passed it to me and I also read it, and realised that we didn't have a President any more. The President had died. And from then on, life changed. There were no more attacks. After his death, FAA soldiers in Quimbele made contact with us, they came into the bush to give us a letter. I read that letter; in it they said that there should be no more war. So our commanders also wrote a letter back agreeing. And from then on we saw that our top leaders, our generals, were going to meet theirs, and from that we understood that this was really peace, that there would be no more war. I thought, "Now I'm free," because military life is like being in a prison, you can only leave when your commander says you can. So when there was peace I felt more at ease. The demobilisation camps this time round were much better than the last time. We felt it was really peace so we felt more relaxed. There was a very good understanding between the FAA and our forces. My life has changed since peace because now I'm at ease; I'm already depending on myself. So even though I still have this health problem, I feel much better. I came back here to M'banza Congo in November 2002. My mother and my brother were still here. I'd been away from my family for eight years. This was the first time I'd seen my mother since 1995. It was a shock when we saw each other again. They had been very sad about me. They'd already been told that I was dead, some years ago. They held a funeral for me and everything. I didn't know that. Then, when I was in Uige after the war, I managed to send a letter saying I was alive. When he got that letter my brother came to Uige to see me and came back here with the news that I really was alive. I don't feel threatened now that I'm back here. The people here have known me for a very long time. They know that I've been with UNITA, but since the war is over there's no point in them being suspicious of me. I never did any harm here, so now no one is doing harm to me.

♀

Mussende
March 2003

I am 33 years old. I'm from Mussende and I always stayed here during the war, except for last year in January, when they [UNITA] took me to the bush and I spent three months there. We went, 480 of us, in January and we only came back here in May. Before that, we really suffered a lot with the war. The people here never lived in decent conditions, we were always suffering. The worst thing was the lack of medicines, salt, clothes, and food. The population could not go and work in their fields far from here. Anybody who tried to go far away was captured by UNITA. UNITA was all around the town. We had to get our food just nearby, in the surroundings of the town, so there was lots of malnutrition. Because of the miserable conditions lots of people became anaemic, and many died of malnutrition, and shortage of food and salt. Lots of children also died because of the situation. I have three children. One of them became anaemic and his body swelled up, but now he's back to normal. When I was captured, I was hiding amongst some banana trees. When they attacked the town, I was at home.

I went out to try to get across the road and past the river and from there to walk to Malange. But it wasn't possible, so I hid in the banana trees with my children. They found me there at 10 o'clock; they grabbed me and took me with them. Later on they recognised me, they knew that I used to work for the government, cooking for the administrator, so they wanted to kill me, but thank heavens they didn't because peace came and they changed a bit. But if the peace hadn't come I would be dead today. They took us to an area they call Zone 3. I don't know where it was exactly, we just had to walk and keep walking. It was there that I heard that Savimbi had been killed but we couldn't say much there. If you talk too much there they kill you, you just have to obey. Everything that they tell you, you do.

After peace came, they didn't want to let us go. They said we had to wait there with them until they went to the demobilisation camps. Only then could we leave. I went with them to the demobilisation camp. I spent two days there and on the third day I came back here, to town. My children were with me the whole time. They are seven, five and three years old. The eldest one had to walk; the other two I carried the whole way, one on my back and one in my arms. We suffered in so many different ways because of the war. If you tried to travel, you'd run into landmines on the road, or they'd attack the cars. You couldn't travel at all; you had to stay just in one place. Life has changed because of peace. Now people are free, they can do what they want. We can travel from one place to another, and because of that, life has improved. Here life is still difficult because of the situation of the roads. All of the bridges on the roads that lead here have been destroyed, cars and trucks cannot get here, so it's harder for us to feel the effects of peace here than in some other places. But we don't want to think about the war any more, we just want to think about our life in the future. With peace everything is going to get better. In a war you can't do anything, but with peace everything is possible.

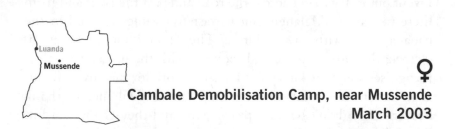

Cambale Demobilisation Camp, near Mussende
March 2003

I am 38 years old. I'm from Cuito; I left there in 1976 because of the war. After our country was invaded [by the Cubans] we thought we'd better withdraw into the bush. When the Cubans entered Huambo, we withdrew into the villages. I didn't go back to Cuito until 1992. Then I went back to the bush when the war started again. We went from there to Caculama, then to Bailundo, and when the government launched their Operation Restoration [in 1999] we had to leave again. We went back to the bush and stayed there until peace came. My life has been very affected by the war. In the first phase, when we were in Jamba, it wasn't so bad but since Restoration it's been really bad; the children couldn't study at all. I have seven children. I have already sent four of them to Luanda to stay with my mother. I have three here with me. But I want to send them to Luanda too because I can see that they're not learning very much in their lessons here. I don't feel the effects of the war much any more. Now, I just want to think about the future of my children. The children are getting used to a normal environment now, they're adapting. Before they used to play games about the war, but they don't any longer. My life hasn't changed much yet, even with peace. Life is still difficult. We came from the bush to here, but here we have received virtually nothing, so we have to keep struggling to try and accumulate something. There have been some changes – there's calm now, people can sleep and wake up when they like, then make a plan for the day and actually realise that plan. They can go out and about because now there are no problems. I think that peace has come to stay because the other times we saw that it was necessary to have UN forces here to enforce the peace, but this time the peace agreement that was reached in Luena[65] was a huge surprise for us. And seeing how things are going, we think this peace will last.

---

[65] The initial cease-fire agreement of March 2002 was signed by the chiefs of staff of UNITA and the FAA in the eastern city of Luena.

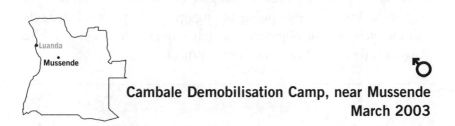

Cambale Demobilisation Camp, near Mussende
March 2003

I am 37 years old. I'm from Benguela. I last left there in 1992 when the war started up again; I'd already been with UNITA. When the Bicesse Accords happened, I went home but then when the war started again, I had to go back to the bush. I first joined UNITA in 1989, out of political conviction – I agreed with the nationalist cause. My life has definitely been affected by the war. This war has affected everybody. This was a guerrilla war, and everyone who knows guerrilla warfare knows that it has many consequences. We all lost our families, on our side and on the other side. In the exchanges of fire all of our families died. There were many sacrifices but since it was all to liberate our country, I consider them normal. My life hasn't changed with peace. We were expecting that the government would support us in the ways that they promised. They said they would give us money but they haven't. They haven't done anything at all that they promised. Of all the things that were written in that Memorandum of Understanding they have done precisely nothing, and today the government is forcing people to leave the demobilisation camps, but that's not what was agreed. For example here, in our camp, we're really abandoned. We've had only two or three food distributions in 10 months. We're only surviving by our own efforts. The life we have here is virtually the same as the way we used to live in the bush. The women have to go and sell their labour to the locals to struggle to earn some little food to eat. Still, I think this peace has come to stay. None of these people will go back to the bush; our leaders are already in Luanda. This time is different from the previous times because the mindset of the Angolan people has changed considerably. Today, in Luanda, people who yesterday couldn't bear to hear about democracy are talking about democracy. Today we're free to listen to [independent] Radio

Ecclesia. So a lot has already changed and we don't need to fight any more. Instead we're going to engage in the political struggle until we achieve our objective – which is to govern Angola. We're Angolans (laughs). We want to take power.

Demining on the outskirts of Malange. Most mines here were laid and booby trapped by UNITA. Malange 2004.

Cuimba
March 2003

I lived in Congo from 1976 to 1991 but when this last war started I didn't have time to get away to Congo. But, we had to run away from the war. The war was very complicated here, a lot of people died. There was fighting here inside Cuimba in 1998 and 1999. In 1999, I ran away to a village and stayed there for a year. Once, in 1999, I was captured by UNITA and they wanted to send me to join their army. I can tell you, I wasn't happy; I was really scared. But I was lucky because I'm a nurse, and while I was with them a woman went into labour and was having trouble giving birth to her baby. I managed to help her, and when they saw that they told me I could stay here and carry on working as a nurse. From then on I wasn't so frightened of them any more. They left me alone so I gave up on the idea of escaping to Congo. I've been here ever since.

War destroys everything. This last war was worse than the other ones. There was too much fighting. My life hasn't changed much since peace. You know, after such a struggle, things can't get better immediately, they change little by little. But we're still a little sad about this peace. For example, we're working here in this clinic under very difficult circumstances, but we're paid next to nothing. This country is really rich and our salaries are minimal. That's not right, it's not good enough. This Province [Zaire] produces petroleum, but we're living here without electricity, without running water. We're not living like people who come from a rich country, and we can't help thinking about that. It's up to the authorities to change things. Since peace has finally come they need to do something to make the people happy. If a person is living in his own house, he should not suffer a lot. This is our land, it's our country; we should be able to live well here, to be happy, and to earn a decent wage. It makes me sad that after one year of peace there is virtually no sign of things changing in this town. Nothing has been fixed up; everything that was old and broken is still old and broken. This clinic here still hasn't been rehabilitated. A lot of people are suffering and dying because there aren't enough medicines. This makes us a bit sad about our peace. In peace we need to think about the future, but we still don't have a decent school here. It shouldn't take so long to do these things. Things have changed a bit since peace. We can travel around now without difficulty, that's already a step in the right direction. For me, peace means happiness for everyone. Without peace you cannot be happy. Now we can think about the future, dream about the future. During the war we could only dream about more war. You know how it is – if someone puts you in a fire, all you can think about is fire. That's what war is like. We hope that this peace will last until the end of time.

Luanda

Mussende

⚥

Cambale Demobilisation Camp, near Mussende
March 2003

This man had recently been reunited with his son after a separation of over 15 years. The son, whose testimony follows, had travelled to Mussende from Mavinga after receiving a Red Cross letter informing him of the whereabouts of his parents.

I'm 50 years old. I'm from Huambo. I left there in 1976 when the Cubans invaded. I've been moving around the interior of the country in the bush ever since, with UNITA. The situation forced us to just keep walking. We suffered a bit. The worst thing was the long walks, and then this last offensive which was really bad. The food situation got really serious; we had no food because the enemy destroyed our crops. I have eight children. But two of our sons, the eldest two, we left behind for them to study. We were going to an area where there were no schools so we left them behind. We left them in Mavinga in the school, and when they'd finished studying they had to stay there. It's only now, after 15 years, that we've met up with one of them again. Fifteen years. In fact it was 15 years and 15 days since we'd seen him. The elder one we still haven't seen but we've heard that he's alive. We used to get news of him occasionally, maybe once a year, until 1998, but since then we'd never heard anything from either of them until 2002.

Before I joined UNITA I was already in the Portuguese colonial army, from 1973. So I already knew military life. I was a mechanic and driver. My father was also a mechanic; he used to teach mechanics in a technical school in Huambo. I can do a bit of farming, a bit of carpentry. So I hope I'll be able to get by in this new life, this new tomorrow. So far our lives haven't changed much since peace. We still have to struggle to find enough to eat. The only difference from before is that there's no more war, there's no more running away all the time. And I have my son back. This peace will definitely last. This is the third time we've had a quartering and demobilisation process but the other times there had to be a peace-keeping force who came from abroad. But this time no, this time we've been here for nine months, and here we're just Angolans. This was the peace we were waiting for. It had to be just between Angolans. Before, the foreigners came to say, "Hey – don't do this, don't do that." But this time it's different. Now I want to go back to the land of my birth, to Huambo.

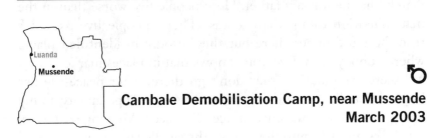

Cambale Demobilisation Camp, near Mussende
March 2003

I'm 23 years old. I was born in Jamba and I always stayed in that area. I grew up there and studied there in the Polyvalent College of UNITA. I had to leave there in 2000 and go to the east because of the military action. But I went back there after the war and that's where I received the letter from my father, which came through the Red Cross, which made me come here to this place in search of them. I studied until the ninth class, when I was 20. Then I was in the army, in the infantry. We were fighting in that area until peace came, and then we went to the demobilisation camp near Mavinga. The war there wasn't too intensive, it wasn't too close. People lived alright, not like in the other areas. I was living there with one of my father's brothers. The last time I saw my parents was in 1988. When I got here and I met them, I didn't believe that it was them (laughs). Only after four or five days did I accept that it was really them because everyone had changed so much. My little brothers whom I last saw when they were three and five, now they're 18 and 20. Some of the others I'd never even met, I just met them now when I came here. For me the worst thing in the war was the fact that we were always moving, we couldn't live in one place for a long time. And there were many, many families who were separated like us. That was very painful…very painful.

I got the letter from my father on February 1, 2003. On February 5, I set off to come and find him. I travelled by aeroplane to Menongue, then from Menongue I took a truck to Huambo and from Huambo to here. The journey took me 15 days because of the state of the roads and the problems of transport. When I got here my mother didn't even recognise me. Only my father recognised me. I always used to imagine my father, thinking he's like this, he's tall, he's whatever. So when I saw him I knew immediately that he was my father. Here people live worse than in the demobilisation camp where I was. There, people live okay. It's true there are mines there but they're only in identified places where nobody goes. Everyone knows that in places marked by an "x" there are mines so they don't go there. After peace life has improved a bit, before I'd never seen a single Angolan city, in my whole life. But now, since peace, I've seen Menongue, Cuito, Huambo, and I'm getting to know the smaller towns as well. And I can see that in the towns and cities people live well, they live better than we did in the bush. I would like to be able to study a bit more now. This peace has come to stay because now many families are being reunited, before, this never happened. And now it's easy for someone to travel wherever he wants to go.

While the son is talking, the father receives another Red Cross letter from his brother in Lubango, whom he hasn't seen or heard from since 1992.

♀
Cuimba
March 2003

I was born in Cuimba. I'm 28 years old. I spent all of the war here. When we ran away it was just to the bush near here. When we heard that UNITA was already close by, when we heard the *tat-a-tat-a boom boom*, we would gather up lots of things, pick up that plate, pick up that bowl, "Ay ay, they're coming, they're coming.

Let's run away," with your child on your back and the rain coming down. We would walk and walk and arrive in the bush and hide in a ravine. We'd climb in there and bend over like this (squats on the floor with her head on her knees) and when UNITA arrives it's *tat-a-tat-a-tat*, and you're bent over like this so that the bullets pass over your head. You crouch there and the children are crying but you stay until the shooting is over. But it's raining and the rain won't stop and the ravine is filling up with water, *glug-a-glug-a-glug*, the water is coming and you have to run from the water as well. *Ay ay ay*, water, more water, and *vooom*, your things are swept away with the water; and *vooom*, your child is taken by the water, but you can't run because of the shooting. So then you hear that the shooting has stopped and you decide that you can't stay here because UNITA is too close. You have to find somewhere else to sleep. It's night and you're walking along, people fall down holes, they get lost in the bush in the night, the children can't keep up, the children get sick. You find some long grass and you put that sick child in there to hide him, and you think, tomorrow, when the shooting's over, we'll come back and find this child. But by the time you get back those bugs that live in the bush have bitten the child; they bite and bite, the child's almost dead. You pick it up and run and run, but where is the medicine, where is the salt, where is the food? In the bush, all you can do is take a special kind of stick, beat it and beat it, mix it with water, it's so bitter, but you make the child drink it. The children's hair goes really red because they can't eat properly.[66] You go and look for bees. You can't be afraid because if you are, you will die of hunger. You follow those bees and find their home and gather lots of leaves and stuff them around their home, take a match, and burn those leaves. With lots of smoke the bees get drunk, *zzzz*, *zzzz*, they come out, they fly around, and if you look inside their house you'll find honey. You take that honey, but while you're doing it the bees are biting you. You can't run because if you do the hunger will catch you. So you're taking the honey thinking, "Ay, ay I'm going to die," and the bees are drunk and biting, *ti-ti-ti*, and when you finish your eyes are big like this, and your lips are all swollen. But at least you have honey. You're there with someone who hasn't eaten for days,

---

[66] A sign of protein deficiency.

he's getting weak, he's groaning. But who's going to look after him? You're also in no state to worry about other people, and the soldiers are still shooting. Everyone's crying, "Hunger, hunger, I'm hungry." Then there's not so much shooting, and we hear that the government have taken Cuimba, that soon they will come to the bush to collect the people. So we say, "Don't cry any more. Soon we'll be in Cuimba. We'll eat food with salt. There will be medicines." But it's too late because this person had four children, and now they're all dead.

One whole year we lived like that. The first wars were just little. But this last one, from 1998, I saw it all. The first time this last war came, we were here, we heard that UNITA were coming out of the bush into the town. We thought "Now what should we do? Let's run to the Congo." The people who had money were buying some food to take with them on the journey, but we didn't have any money, nothing in our hands. We know that in Congo you have to dig in your pocket to pay for everything and we couldn't pay. So we stayed here. We stayed and stayed and stayed. Then UNITA came and attacked Cuimba. We gathered our things and fled along that road (points north). Run, run, run, and we arrive in a village over there. The next day, really early, UNITA came there. They said "Don't be afraid, we haven't come to kill the people, we haven't come to kill you. You must go back to Cuimba, go back home, we won't do anything to you." And we're thinking "Ah, is it true? They won't hurt us?" So UNITA is mobilising the people, saying "Come, come, all of you come. We aren't going to do anything to you." So we all asked ourselves and asked each other, what should we do? And we decided to return to Cuimba with them. We got back here, but so many people had gone to the Congo. We were afraid to stay alone, each in our own house, so we all went to one place in the middle of the town. And there we are and we hear *hmmmmmmm*, that thing they call a MIG, *hmmmmmmm*, *DUM DUM DUM DUM*. And we cry "Ay, ay, ay, ay, what should we do?" And here comes another one, *hmmmmmm DUM DUM DUM*, dropping bombs from the sky. And one person says, "It's ok, it's a passenger plane, it's ok." and another says, "No it's not, it's the government, come to kill the people." Ay, ay and what should we do? These bombs kill people and the wind that they make, it kills people too – they drop poison. We wonder, "Should we run back to the villages? But then UNITA will come there to fetch us again." And then we're hungry, and it's already three o'clock in the afternoon, and we think that the MIGs won't come back again today, so we decide to cook. We're all so scared. And then at six o'clock *hmmmmm*, again, and some people hide in the houses, some hide under the bed, some hide in the long grass, some hide in the bathroom, and *DUM DUM DUM DUM* they're bombing from way up high. Fear. You pick up your child and you run, you have to dig a hole, a big hole like a grave, you dig and dig and then each person hides in their hole. As soon as you hear the planes you run to your hole with your child and you jump in there, you don't climb down carefully, you just jump, and cover your nose and mouth and try not to breathe so that poison doesn't get inside. And those bombs, they make hundreds of small sharp things. Like if you take this glass (picks up a drinking glass) and you drop it on the floor, it breaks and makes lots of small sharp things. That's what the bombs make and those things they destroy people. If you're running and the bomb falls before you reach your hole those sharp things, cut you here and cut you there. Ay, ay, ay. So that's when we ran away to the bush. Most of this last war we were hiding in the bush. When UNITA comes and shoots, we run to another place. And when the government comes and shoots, we run to another place. And they're both wandering around saying, "Where are the people?" You can't light a fire during the day, only at night, so that they won't see the smoke and find you. UNITA wants to kill the FAA. And the FAA wants to kill UNITA. We're not FAA or UNITA but the guns don't know that, the bullets don't choose who they hit. You have to run away or you'll die.

I came back to Cuimba in 2002. Until then I was always in the bush. Then, in 2002, we heard that the government had taken Cuimba, so the MIGs weren't bombing Cuimba any more. And the government was going into the bush, gathering up the people, and taking them to Cuimba. And we were there with so much hunger wondering when is the government going to come and get us; how can we let them know we're here? So we decide we're not going to cook at night any more. We're going to cook during the day and make a big fire with lots of smoke, and when the govern-

ment sees the smoke they will know there are people here. We've
already had enough of dying of hunger. That's the worst thing in
war – so much death. This woman had three children and now
she's alone, she has no children. You think that you'll go to your
fields to fetch some food to feed your children and then you hear
that UNITA is there, they're sitting in your fields, eating your
food, eating it until it's all gone. You can't go there, you're hiding
from UNITA. So we made a fire and the government came and
found us and we're all crying, "Hunger, hunger," and the government says that the suffering is over and we're all going back to
Cuimba together to start eating properly again. We gather up our
things, we put them on our heads, we walk through the bush,
across these mountains, and we come to Cuimba. And here in
Cuimba no one works, we just eat and eat but then we hear
rumours that UNITA is coming again. They're coming back to
attack Cuimba, and *ay, ay* we don't want to be here when they
attack, their bullets won't choose between us and the soldiers. We
want to run and hide in the bush, but the government doesn't
want us to. We're their people now, they came to get us in the
bush and now we have to stay in the town. If they catch us running away they will fight us. So at night we leave all of our things
in our houses, we take nothing, and we close our doors to make it
look like we're there sleeping, and we creep away to hide in the
bush in a place where their bullets won't reach us. And then we
hear that Savimbi is dead. Can it be true? Yes, he's dead. Peace,
peace, peace. Is it really peace or what? God has to help us to
make it real peace. Not peace like before where you're lying in
your bed and then you hear *BOOM*, and you leap out of bed and
gather up all your things and you don't sleep any more. You spend
the rest of the night sitting on a chair, trying to stay awake listening, listening for the shooting, in case you have to run. And the
next day, nobody goes to the river to fetch water, nobody goes to
the fields. You have no appetite, you don't want to eat, you're too
nervous, you're thinking too hard, your head hurts, your heart is
racing. How are you going to eat when you're like that? But then
three days go by with no shooting, four days, a week, and we're
still okay. It's peace. When your child cries you can leave him to
cry, you don't have to shut him up out of fear. Or you can go down

to the river, or to the fields, and you're not afraid of being caught by soldiers. It's peace and life is different. We are dressing well; when people are sick they can receive proper treatment; when a woman's having trouble giving birth, the doctors can take her to the hospital in M'banza Congo in a car. Before, if you had trouble in childbirth, you would just die. The only way to get to the hospital was on a stretcher. Three or four days on a stretcher, with that motion, *chucka-chucka-chuck*, of course you're going to die. In the war nobody could sleep well. Now we can sleep well. In the war, even if it was really hot in your house, you had to sleep wearing three skirts and five shirts, and then if you heard tat-a-tat-a-tat you could run to the bush with those clothes on your body and those clothes would help you to survive. Now, you can sleep with no clothes on if you like. You can wake up whenever you like, you can sleep until eight o'clock if you want. During the war, four o'clock in the morning and your sleep was over because that was the hour of the attacks – that was the hour of danger. You had to be awake then. You'd sit, with your heart beating fast, drunk with fear and thinking, until nine o'clock, waiting to see if an attack was coming, and then your heart would start to slow down little by little. Now, we can sleep. We can sing loudly. We can go to the city without fear. With peace, people can work; the children are going to school. Peace has to last.

🜨
Demobilized UNITA soldier
Bié
June 2003

I was in the bush for over 30 years with UNITA. I am proud to say that, of all of my family, no one came to serious harm in the war. Shortly before the war ended, I was taken as a prisoner of war. At this point, I was weak from having lived so long in the bush without food and without salt. I had oedema and it took me until April 2002 to recover. The FAA did not mistreat me, they just took our things, like clothes and blankets, but our main interest was staying alive, so we just kept our mouths shut. Later, the FAA asked me to work for them, but after so many years of military service, I had suffered enough. Since I refused, they wanted me to go to an *aquartelimento* [Quartering and Family Area] but I had already been in *aquartelimentos* in 1992 and 1996. These places were really isolated and everyone living there had been subject to abuses from the FAA. So I just didn't want to go there again. They let me go free...and I settled here with my family. All the *bairros* are made up of people who used to be on the UNITA side and emerged from the bush after the war. When everyone was returning, they were registered by the government in town, and this information was shared with the town administration, the government and MINARS [*Ministério de Assistência e Reinserção Social*] – which are really all the same – as well as with the local *soba* [traditional leader] and with the WFP. This means all the people registered by the government come under their control. The registration process is so public that everyone knows who came into town from the bush, and who is demobilized. I was registered by the government and by the WFP, but I don't have a demobilization card because I did not go to the *aquartelimento*. But MINARS did register me for a one-time subsidy and gave me clothes for the children. It was a big fight for many months to obtain all the different documents—we had to invest money and dip into our savings so I could work again. Most people who came back here from the bush don't have any form of identification—meaning there is no proof that they are Angolan citizens. I think that without the official knowledge of the government, the police use this to their advantage in the *bairros*. They go to the people they know are demobilized and search for documents they often don't have—and then make trouble for them.

There was a man who was a demobilized soldier from Chicala Reception Area [Moxico province]. On June 4, two policemen had been drinking a lot and they went to this man's house. They called his wife to ask her for a light for their cigarettes. Then they told her to call her husband and asked him for all his documents, and he actually had everything. These two policemen took all the papers with them, as well as the man's wife, but they gave no explanation as to why. The man didn't know what to do. I told him to talk to the police, the town administration, MINARS – but all of these are the government – where else could he go? I didn't know what to tell him. Is this supposed to be peace? Is this supposed to be liberty? In the end, the man was just too afraid. We have no news of the woman or of this man's papers since that time. And this is just the newest example. The government has promised security for the demobilized. We need protection, and I am not sure they will protect us. And for me, security is the foundation for everything else we need, like food, health or schooling. The last of all will be development. For right now, my safety is my mouth, keeping my mouth shut.

Returning refugee from DRC
Luau transit centre, Moxico province
July 2003

My sister and I fled to the DRC in 1998 when the war broke out again. We had travelled from our home in Luacano to buy salt in Luau. But on our way back, the fighting started when we reached Cavungo, so we fled across the border to Congo. The war was terrible. There was no food – we needed all of you [NGOs], otherwise we never would have survived. After 2000, there was no more food distribution in Divuma camp [in DRC], so we had to work to eat. You could work your own fields one day, then also work for other people. Then you could buy fish to eat at the market. This year, UNHCR started to go among the people and let us know that if we had it in our hearts to go home, we could return. We left because we could never find sufficient work. We suffered a lot in the camp and many people left the camp to live outside. My family stayed because everyone said the war would end someday and we hoped to get transport to go back if we stayed in the camp. So several months ago, we signed up to return. The journey went well, only one of the children got sick. I have been thinking a lot about my life and which way to go. We really depend on what you [NGOs] say, whether UNHCR says a place is acceptable or not, whether the road is safe, or whether the area is mined. We will stay here if they say that is better, but we will leave for Luacano if they give us word that it is safe to go. We have nothing to say, I am a refugee and am waiting for the word from UNHCR. We now have no other family here in Luau. My father died near Luacano during the war. My mother died in 2001 in DRC. When I was in Divuma, I decided it was better not to be alone, so I married. I also have a brother in Luanda. I wrote two messages to him and I am waiting for him to send me word whether I should go to Luanda from here. I think I could earn a living in Luanda by fishing. Until I hear from my brother, we will build a house here and then look for work. I could also stay here [in the transit centre] a little longer until things are clear. But it's not for me to say I want this or I want that. In the end, God will tell me what to do. Otherwise nothing will succeed.

⚲
Kunje transit centre, Bié
August 2003

I am not leaving with the transport today. I am still waiting for my wife who stayed in Mavinga with our children. I came here to see the situation and I will go back to pick her up next month. Then we will travel here together. When we were still together in the bush, she and I were separated during an attack on December 13, 2001. She was captured and I never saw her again until we found each other in Mavinga this May. That was a forced separation but now we are reconciled. I originally left home in 1977 and I lived for 27 years in Jamba – it was so big. When the war ended, everything was destroyed. We left everything behind and no one had anything after the cease-fire. When we arrived in Matungo, so many people were dying, all the fields looked like a cemetery, and they were burying people just like animals. The government did not keep its promises, but finally in July 2002, MSF showed up, and then the WFP. If it were not for MSF and the WFP, we would never have had anything to eat. This March, they told us that we were going to leave the *aquartelimento* so we had one month to prepare for our departure. In April, we left by car to Mavinga, then went by plane to Menongue, then from there to Cuito by car. We arrived here on August 13. When we were still in Matungo, there were people there from all over – Benguela, Huila, Huambo, and so those of us from the Umbundu [speaking] part decided to leave together.

I received the complete kit, but the money they promised, 6350 kwanza, is missing. My wife is the one who has the WFP card, so I have never received rations myself. Also, I never received a tent or plastic sheeting, which was promised, and now my old tent from 2002 is falling apart and the rains are already starting. I am not sure how we are supposed to eat with neither money, nor food, nor a WFP card. But we hear from other places like Huambo that people receive a monthly ration. Here, the WFP made a list but we never received ration cards. When we don't have shelter and we don't eat either, people get sick. This is dying, sleeping badly out here in the wind with these tents. Two people just died here today.

2004 © Kadir van Lohuizen

Internally displaced people (IDPs) still live in old UN tents in Viana, just outside Luanda. Viana 2004.

It is clear we are meant to suffer before we reach our place of origin. Another problem is water. They shut down the wells a few times a day, I think so the water can be replenished. But then when we try to use the hand-pumps in the *bairros*, people ask us for money or they tell us it's a government well and we have no right to that water. They say "Savimbi left nothing behind, all the water went into his belly." Because of this problem with the hand-pumps, they beat up one of the children last week. What we need here is a leader or a representative to resolve our problems, and to bring our concerns higher up. If we go to MINARS, they send us away saying "well, you fought us." If we go to the police, our problems stay there and are not resolved. We would prefer an alliance with the police because we are returning to stay here for a long time. But what has the government done? When we left here, this factory we're living in was functioning but now it is destroyed and the government has done nothing to get it running.

As for our health, we are not getting the full doses of drugs here in the hospital. Those who are here longer get better treatment than the new arrivals. And the personnel treat some people better than others especially when it is their family here in the transit centre. It was similar in Matungo, where there were almost no medications and we used to have to go into the bush for medicines. Right now, my main concerns are money, the things I need, like blankets, a tent and medications, and finally getting my documents in order. Now that the war is over and there is peace, I want to lead a normal life. I want to just take my papers and go to Moxico, Luanda or wherever I want.

Cuando Cubango
October 2003

It was in 1974 that I left home for the bush to join UNITA and ended up in Cuando Cubango. In 1988, I had a mine accident which injured my leg. When the war ended, I travelled to the border with an FAA transport to find my family who had gone to Namibia to take one of our children to the hospital in Rungo. I arrived there in March 2002, but our child had died. We didn't have money, so we needed to stay there until I could afford transport back here. There wasn't much movement, so I had to find a private car. When we arrived in Menongue in September, I went to MINARS to register and to get transportation back to Bié, but I am still waiting. They told me to stay here until they could arrange transportation. The same night, before we came out here, they gave us each a can of rice, but nothing more. And we never had any further information from MINARS except that we were to stay here.

I am an IDP. I am not demobilized because I was never in the *aquartelimento*, and never received documents. I am also not a refugee because I don't have those documents; I only have a *laissez-passer* from Namibia. I am doing everything I can now to get a WFP card, but I am not sure if I will get one. It is hard to get access to the people who make the decisions about this. Food is my main concern at the moment. Then, we also need clothes and things like cooking utensils or blankets. Other people here are giving us food because they feel sorry for us suffering hunger. We may have a health post here, but since there is no food, it is so hard to recover. I don't know if my family can stay here in these conditions. So now I am looking for a way to get back to Bié. I was thinking about returning to Likua, but I think none of the people I knew are still there. My wife is originally from Menongue and has family who knows we are here, so we will stay here until we have more information about my family in Bié so we can return. I hope to find my brother. The last time I saw him was in 1974, when he left for the north and I left for the south of Angola. The main thing we would like for the future is information so we can decide what to do and then we get the transportation to go back.

I'm 18 years old. I was born right here. I left here in 1998. Until then I had always lived here. Life here was pretty normal; except for the threats from UNITA, and the fear. UNITA used to wait for the people in the fields. People were scared to go to the fields; you couldn't go there alone in case you'd meet UNITA on the way. If you met them they'd either take you or they'd kill you. That already happened to some people I know. For some years UNITA lived here in the town too. They used to ask who belonged to the MPLA and who belonged to UNITA, and lots of people died because of that. If they thought someone liked the MPLA, they would steal their things and at night they would take the people away. There was lots of fear. My parents were always afraid, but I was okay, I used to sleep well here. We couldn't travel where we wanted then, we couldn't go and fetch anything we wanted, we had to wait here.

In 1998, I went to Luanda because they were rounding up the girls here. UNITA used to take them to put them in JURA. My father thought it was best to get me out of here so he sent me to Luanda. I went alone, my parents stayed here. And there, I stayed with my cousin. I went to school. It was nice. I stayed there five years and I just came back here a month ago. My parents and my brothers and sisters had a bad time here during the war. They had no clothes, they couldn't go to school. I came back because my parents were missing me and they wanted me back. And also because here the school is free; no one has to pay money to go to school. In Luanda you need money to go to school, and I was there alone, I didn't have money. So it was better to come here. Now I'm going to school here. I think Mussende is fine. It will develop, little by little. It's very different from Luanda, but it will get better. They'll fix up all the things that are broken and it will be beautiful. My life has changed because of peace. Now I'm here with people who I didn't imagine I'd be able to see again. Now, if you need to go and fetch something, you can travel freely, without fear. I want to study, to get a good job, to be able to help my parents.

🜂

13-year-old boy
Mussende
March 2003

I've always lived in Mussende. The war here...I can't tell you...we suffered a lot. We had to sleep in the bush, to walk in the rain, to sleep on leaves, because of the war. We were running away from war, from attacks, they were attacking the people. I don't know why. No one could leave the town. The fields were occupied by UNITA troops. If you went from here, even as far as that hill over there (points to a hill about one kilometre away), they would kill you. We had no food. We had to pick the mangoes from these trees, or dig up the potatoes that we could grow between the houses. We were so hungry, you can't imagine. We all got terrible diarrhoea. So many people died here. One day 15 people would die, another day 30 or 50. They died from hunger. I only survived with God's help, thank God. None of my family died of hunger. It's just my father who died; he died from the war. They shot him inside our house. It was UNITA. He hadn't done anything. I was there. So many things happened in the war.

Life has definitely changed since the war ended. There's no more war, there's just laughter. Life's better. We can sleep well, move about normally, there's no problem with food. There's no more fear. But at night I still dream that there's more war. Many times, I dream about soldiers and attacks and running away. And if a helicopter or a plane goes by I get a fright, I think there's more war coming. We had lots of planes, MIGs, helicopters here, many things, bombing, here in the town. I think that peace has come, so that we can live very well. I want to study now.

During the war I could never study. I've just started now for the first time. I like it but I can't read and write yet. The war ruined Angola a lot. All of the houses are broken, the bridges, everything. We don't want any more war.

♀
13-year-old girl
Cuimba
March 2003

I was born in the Congo, in a camp. I lived with my mother and my father there. Now I am living here with my mother and my father is in M'banza Congo. I came here to go to school. We came in a car not long ago, this year. I don't know what month. We came with my mother and my brothers and sisters, and my father stayed behind in the city. I like Cuimba; I prefer it here because we're studying well here. I never went to school before. I know war; I saw the war. I saw the shooting. I was in the bush as well, with UNITA, not far from here. We came back from the Congo and then we went into the bush; for a long time. My father was working there in the bush; he was a soldier with UNITA. There was nothing for me to do in the bush. We used to carry things. There were weapons, guns. But I wasn't afraid there, I'm not afraid of war. At the end of the war we left the bush and we went to the demobilisation camp. We ate food out of tins there (laughs). I liked that. My father is demobilised now. War is not good. Every day you have to carry things and walk. Lots of people die. I know that Angola is at peace now, but I don't really know what I think about it. I'm not sure what peace is.

ठ
12-year-old boy
Cuimba
March 2003

I was born in Congo, in a town called Kimpese. When we left there, we came here to Angola in a car. We went to our village and we stopped there for a while, but then the war came and we ran away to the bush. Afterwards, we had to carry things on our heads every day. We were running every day, carrying our things. Then the war ended and we came here to Cuimba. In the bush we were with UNITA. Then the FAA came into the bush to fetch us and bring us here. In the war I saw weapons and lots of things.... Our village is called Sango. UNITA came there and took the people with them to the bush. I went with my mother and my father. We were there a long time. We thought that there would never be peace in Angola. We thought the war would never end. The FAA came into the bush and they brought us to Cuimba. I don't know what year it was. We've been here since then. War is not good. Every day it's just fighting. My life has changed because of peace. Now there's no more fear that the war will come back, it's over. And now I'm going to school, that's because of peace. We're going to school but we have no books, no pencils, and the teachers don't get paid. There's not going to be more war, it won't come back again. I don't know what I want to be when I grow up. I don't want to be a soldier.

Luanda
Mussende

♀
10-year-old girl
Mussende
March 2003

I'm living here with my uncle. My parents are in their fields. It's quite far away. I've been here since last April. Before, I was in the pre-school class and now I'm in the first class. I've never seen the war. When the war came here we left. We walked that way (pointing north) to Malange. We stayed there a month. Then we went to Luanda. We've been in Luanda a long time. One of my brothers died there, of sickness. Another is still there. Here there are four of us. We're living with our uncle so we can go to school. Peace is when the war is over. When peace came my mother said "There's too much sickness in Luanda, we're going home." And so we came back here.

2004 © Kadir van Lohuizen

The Malange market. Malange 2004.

"Peace has to last."

A Closing Word

One cannot overestimate the reward of war's end, of the lifting of violence from the shoulders of an entire society. The challenges ahead, however, are colossal. Cities, towns and villages; roads, railways and bridges; schools and hospitals – everything has been in tatters. The rural economy has been destroyed, with commercial farming virtually non-existent. And to complicate reconstruction, the country is still sown with landmines. Roads and bridges cannot be rebuilt, and fields cannot be cleared for planting until they have first been cleared of mines. In a country the size of Angola the task of de-mining will take generations.

The task of repairing the social and emotional wounds inflicted by the conflict is also likely to take generations. In the short term, half a million UNITA men, women and children somehow have to be reintegrated into the lives of towns and villages which they may have helped to attack, uproot, and destroy. In the long term, the country's entire social fabric needs time to recover. Angola's war lasted for 42 years. Average life expectancy in Angola is now around 45 years. This means that the great majority of Angolans have only ever known war. They have grown up and grown old in an environment of constant uncertainty, of fear and increasingly, of despair. Living constantly under threat takes a heavy toll, both physically and emotionally. It will take more than a few years of fragile peace to heal the profound emotional wounds inflicted by a lifetime of war. This essential healing process will not be helped by the fact that many Angolans have been left without the support and comfort of their families and communities. As these stories have shown, across the country, families have been torn apart by the war; whole villages have been wiped off the map; generations have never set eyes on the villages which their parents call home.

It is up to the Angolan government to take the lead in meeting these challenges and to show that it places the welfare of its citizens above all other considerations.

"In a war you can't do anything, but with peace everything is possible."

Carnival in Luanda. Luanda 2004.

2004 © Kadir van Lohuizen

Annex 1
Chronology of Events

1956	MPLA (Popular Movement for the Liberation of Angola) founded
1961	Armed struggle against Portuguese colonial rule begins
1966	UNITA (National Union for the Total Independence of Angola) founded
1974	Fascist regime in Portugal overthrown. The new Portuguese government begins the process for Angolan independence.
11/1975	Angola gains independence from Portugal. MPLA declares itself the government. Rival nationalist groups claim a share of power and civil war ensues. South African forces come to fight alongside UNITA; Cuban forces come to fight alongside the MPLA.
1976	MPLA and Cuban troops capture the UNITA stronghold of Huambo. UNITA is forced into the bush and begin the "long march" which culminates in the foundation of a new headquarters in Jamba.
1979	MPLA President, Agostinho Neto dies. He is replaced as head of the MPLA, and President of Angola, by José Eduardo dos Santos.
1986	The United States government welcomes UNITA leader Jonas Savimbi to the White House and gives millions of dollars of military assistance to UNITA.
12/1988	With the end of the Cold War, Cuba and South Africa both agree to withdraw their forces from Angola. UNITA and the MPLA continue to fight each other.
5/1991	UNITA and the MPLA sign the Bicesse Accords, ending the Cold War phase of the conflict and agree to hold UN-monitored elections. 1.5 million Angolans are left displaced by the conflict.

9/1992   Legislative and Presidential Elections take place. The MPLA wins more votes than UNITA. UNITA rejects the results. Civil war resumes. UNITA soon controls 70 percent of Angola.

9/1993   UN Security Council imposes arms and fuel embargo on UNITA.

11/1994   The MPLA and UNITA sign the Lusaka Peace Accords, agreeing to a cease-fire and a new, UN-monitored peace process. Two million Angolans are left homeless by the conflict. Four years of fragile peace follow, punctuated by regular military clashes.

8/1997   UN Security Council accuses UNITA of failing to disarm and imposes further sanctions on the movement, banning flights into UNITA territory and all travel by named UNITA officials.

1998   From March onwards, the peace process begins to break down as UNITA forces retake control of areas handed over to state administration during the peace process. A new wave of civilian displacement ensues.

6/1998   UN Security Council holds UNITA responsible for the breakdown of the peace process and imposes further sanctions, banning the purchase of UNITA diamonds and freezing UNITA bank accounts.

12/1998   The final phase of the war begins.

8/1999   The FAA launches a new offensive named Operation Restoration which results in the capture of UNITA's headquarters.

2000   The FAA commences "cleansing"operations to depopulate rural areas and starve UNITA out of the bush.

2/2002   UNITA leader Jonas Savimbi is killed in battle near Lucusse, in Moxico Province.

3/2002   UNITA and the FAA agree to a cease-fire.

4/4/2002   A new peace agreement formally ending the war and agreeing to a new peace process is signed by the two parties in the Angolan capital, Luanda. Hundreds of thousands of starving UNITA supporters begin to emerge from the bush. Four million Angolans, or one third of the population, are displaced and homeless.